The Dawn Warriors

The Dawn Warriors

Man's Evolution Toward Peace

by Robert Bigelow

HUTCHINSON OF LONDON

HUTCHINSON & CO (*Publishers*) LTD
178–202 Great Portland Street, London W1

London Melbourne Sydney
Auckland Bombay Toronto
Johannesburg New York

First published 1969

*Printed in Great Britain by litho on antique wove paper
by Anchor Press, and bound by Wm. Brendon,
both of Tiptree, Essex*

09 100240 0

To my wife

CONTENTS

	Author's Note	ix
I.	COOPERATION-FOR-CONFLICT	3
II.	SOCIALIZED MONKEYS AND APES	21
	Monkeys	22
	Apes	32
III.	HAND-AXE TO H-BOMB	45
IV.	POPULATION EXPLOSIONS	61
	Mesopotamia	62
	Very Ancient Greece	65
	When a Population Explosion Explodes	74
	Ancient Greece	79
	China	84
	American Indians	90
V.	HAREMS AND NATURAL SELECTION	103
	Lebensraum	106
	Polygamy	109
	Mutation	116
	Genetic Drift	121
	Human Diversity	127
	Human Equality	130
	Sheep, Goats, and Natural Selection	134
VI.	CAVALRY AND BATTLESHIPS	137
	Horses	139
	Ships	170
VII.	PREHISTORIC PEACE	183
VIII.	GOLDEN RULES AND PROMISED LANDS	217
IX.	BIOLOGY AND CULTURE	239
X.	COOPERATION-FOR-SURVIVAL	249
	References	257
	Index	263

vii

AUTHOR'S NOTE

EVERY IDEA is a unique combination of remembered concepts and experiences. In this sense, each and every thought is original. But in another sense, no idea is original. All our conceptions are conglomerations of thoughts conceived in other heads before they entered ours. I am therefore deeply in debt to *Homo sapiens* for every combination of thoughts in this book. The debt is greater, however, in the case of certain individuals — some of whom may wish to remain incognito.

The encouragement and editorial advice of Carleton S. Coon, Peter Davison, and my wife and sons, were invaluable.

Colleagues at the University of Canterbury — Professor George A. Knox and other members of the Zoology Department in particular — gave valuable advice and encouragement.

I am also indebted to colleagues who made arrangements for lectures and seminar discussions at the following universities and research institutions: Department of Zoology, University of Hawaii; Department of Entomology, University of Kansas; Laboratory of Genetics, University of Wisconsin; The Rockefeller University, New York; Biology Department, University of Ottawa; Research Branch, Canada Department of Agriculture; Macdonald College of McGill University; Hope Department of Entomology, and Zoology Department, Oxford University; Department of Zoology, Lucknow

University, India; Department of Zoology, University of
Western Australia; Department of Zoology, University of
Adelaide; Department of Genetics, University of Melbourne.

I wish, finally, to thank all those scholars, teachers,
authors, and friends whose interwoven ideas are the conceptual continuum through which we all seek understanding.

The Dawn Warriors

I

COOPERATION-FOR-CONFLICT

A HYDROGEN BOMB is an example of mankind's enormous capacity for friendly cooperation. Its construction requires an intricate network of human teams, all working with single-minded devotion toward a common goal. Let us pause and savor the glow of self-congratulation we deserve for belonging to such an intelligent and sociable species. Without this high level of cooperation no hydrogen bomb could be built. But without an equally high potential for ferocity, no hydrogen bomb ever *would* be built. Perhaps our cooperation has something to do with our ferocity.

In a world teeming with animals whose survival depends on group cooperation, man's lead is unchallenged. In a world where animals rarely slaughter other members of their own species in large numbers, our very impressive record of warfare makes us unique. We are without doubt the most cooperative and the most ferocious animals that have ever inhabited the earth. We are contradictory creatures who expound philosophies which concede on the one hand that we are as ferocious as the

3

evidence suggests, and proclaim on the other that we are "innately peaceful" victims of a corrupt culture. Our capacity for warfare has reached a level we describe as "unthinkable," yet this very capacity to wage a global war means that our social organization has reached a level from which the achievement of a stable world peace is at least feasible.

As Shakespeare put it, "two such opposèd foes encamp us still." When we approach the problems of war and peace, violence and nonviolence, we usually do so as Shakespeare did — on the assumption that war and peace are diametrically opposite to one another, each the very antithesis of the other. In this book I will suggest that these two apparent opposites of human nature are complementary rather than contradictory, and I will propose an explanation of human evolution that considers warfare as the force that demanded a threefold increase in the size of the brain in a mere two or three million years. But I will not hold warfare up as in any way "good" or "necessary," and I will neither propose nor defend an ethical or political doctrine.

Very briefly, the thesis is this:

Early humans were organized in socially cooperative groups, more or less as baboons are organized today, but on a higher level of complexity. The cooperation was almost entirely confined to individuals who belonged to the *same* group. Cooperation *between* groups was virtually nonexistent, and the individuals of each little group regarded all *other* groups — that is, all *foreigners* — as potential threats to their own survival. Effective social cooperation within each group depended very largely on the efficiency of the brains and the endocrine systems in the component individuals. Effective group action, even at a subhuman level, requires effective *communication* between individuals. All communication between animal nervous systems is accomplished through signs and symbols. A particular snort or bark, for example, is not in itself a lion, but it can convey to other brains the information that a lion is not far away. Baboons and dogs and many other animals can convey information to one another at this basic level. But even with baboons and dogs, the brain that receives the sign or symbol must be able to interpret it effectively. Our speech merely agitates the air; brains are required to make sense of these agitations. The words on this page merely produce a pattern of light radiations; human brains are required to resolve these patterns in a meaningful way. The patterns of sound and light waves are merely codes for communication between human brains.

Effective group action, then, required cooperation and communication and *brains* — even before our ancestors became what we would now call human. This social organization and cooperation were required for sheer biological survival, first from the attacks of lions and other large predators, later from the far more dangerous attacks of other human groups. Those groups with the most effective brains, and hence with the greatest capacity for effective cooperation in attack or defense, maintained themselves longest in the most fertile and otherwise desirable areas. In these areas they produced more offspring, and additional groups. Those with the most effective brains and the most efficient in-group cooperation were less often massacred wholesale by other groups, and less often driven into deserts to starve.

Whenever a group with a higher average ability to cooperate exterminated a group with a lower average ability to cooperate — or whenever a large number of closely related groups forced one another to expand outward over a large fertile area, driving out all previous inhabitants who were unable to cooperate well enough to hold their ground — the result was usually a slight increase in the average effectiveness of the human brain over the world as a whole. Occasionally the result would be a slight decrease, but on the average the people with the more effective brains would have prevailed. Evolution is a statistical process that works through the law of averages.

During the entire process no two groups would have been identical genetically, and human brains develop *only* through the action of human sets of genes. No set of chimpanzee genes has ever produced a human brain. The exact number of genes involved is as yet unknown, but I think we can assume that practically every gene in the body is involved in producing a social instrument containing some ten billion nerve cells, each with some 25,000 interconnections, all arranged and organized in a way that can interpret the signs and symbols of a human language. It is not very likely that any two brains are exactly alike — or ever have been. Some can learn social

6

cooperation more quickly, and at a more complex level, than others can. This has always been so.

We have, then, the ingredients required for evolution:

(1) *Genetic variability* is maintained continuously through *recombination*. Whenever an egg is fertilized a new *combination* of human genes begins to interact. This unique combination of genes, given adequate protection against massacre or starvation, will produce a unique human with a unique brain. No other human ever has been or ever will be identical with this individual. There is a continuous rebirth of genetic variability with each new generation of babies, which is what sex is all about.

(2) *Natural selection* takes place when more individuals are produced than can survive. There is then a struggle for survival and the most successful individuals survive to produce the most offspring. In the case of human evolution, success was dependent primarily on the ability to learn social cooperation for defense and offense against threats from other human groups. Those groups who failed to cooperate effectively were either slaughtered wholesale by foreign enemies or driven into deserts where they starved, or barely managed to survive.

Social cooperation, which leads to the Golden Rule and what we call the highest human qualities, was demanded by what we call the lowest of human qualities: the ferocity of human enemies. Shakespeare's two opposèd foes that still encamp us therefore evolved together. They were not even two different sides of the same coin, but were as intimately interdependent as our brains and hearts are. Cooperation was not substituted for conflict. Cooperation-for-conflict, considered as a single, hyphenated word, was demanded — for sheer survival.

As the human brain gradually increased in size and efficiency, people here and there acquired brains enough to see the advantage of *intergroup* cooperation. This was probably very difficult, for it required cooperation with man's most deadly enemy — human foreigners. But as soon as the first two human groups formed a military alliance against a third, the single group that stood alone in its path of advance was in grave peril. When faced with an intergroup alliance of ferocious enemies, defending groups either forgot their feuds and formed an equally powerful counteralliance — or else they suffered the fate of the Canaanite cities in which all who breathed were put to the sword by the twelve allied tribes that followed Joshua and Yahweh into the Promised Land. We are not always fond of foreigners, but there are times when it pays to cooperate with them, when it pays to have brains enough to see the wisdom in the words: "United we stand, divided we fall." When men began to see this wisdom the pace of human evolution quickened. The contending armies became bigger, their weapons became sharper, and the casualties increased accordingly. *But the areas within which relative peace prevailed also increased.* These larger, but still restricted areas of intergroup cooperation gradually expanded. War became bloodier and more intense, but less frequent and less

8

widespread. We are now cooperating more effectively, in more all-embracing terms, than at any other time in the entire history and prehistory of mankind. But we are also deploying intercontinental ballistic missiles with thermonuclear warheads. Our survival as a species may depend on whether or not, *as a species*, we have brains enough to understand the words: "United we stand, divided we fall!"

No theory on the evolution of man can be "proved" in the way mathematical problems are proved. We cannot, in fact, always agree on the very meaning of "proof" — and the *degree* of proof we demand often depends on the intensity of our belief in the proposition under fire. We cannot, in the name of either science or reason, demand absolute proof for unwanted interpretations, nor can we expect to find absolute proof for our own most cherished beliefs. We all sift evidence through the very complicated mesh of our own particular bias. The devout Communist demands absolute proof in enormous quantities before he concedes that capitalism has many good features — and the devout anti-Communist does likewise in reverse order. A pacifist, dedicated to the proposition that all men are "innately peaceful," will place contrary evidence under heavy fire before yielding a particle of his faith. For these reasons I will not attempt to prove my theory in any absolute sense. But I *will* attempt to show that it is based on *evidence* rather than on sheer belief.

The evidence for this theory has not been drawn only from "biology" (in the narrow sense).* I have made forays into the sacred precincts of anthropology, archaeology, sociology, psychology, history, philosophy, and theology. All these studies have a bearing on human evolution, and they cannot be ignored in any really serious attempt to explain it. In the remainder of this chapter, I will try to present this variety of evidence together in one piece, as a whole, in the hope that this will help the reader to appreciate the significance of each subsequent chapter *as he reads it*. This book is not a mystery story, although it does attempt to solve the greatest of all mysteries: the evolution of the human brain. I will try, therefore, to avoid keeping the reader in suspense unnecessarily. I will try to make it as easy as I can for him to see the proposed solution as soon as possible, so that he can better evaluate the evidence for himself as he reads along.

Complex social cooperation is not peculiar to man alone. Many recent studies of baboons and other primates have established beyond all doubt that we are not the only social animals. All monkeys and apes live in social groups. Every species of primate, without exception, is a social species. The groups are always organized socially in a complex dominance hierarchy. Individuals contend with one another for status, but at any one time each one usually "knows his place" and acts accordingly. The dominance structure is constantly changing as the

---

* If man is a living thing, and if biology is the study of living things, then the study of any and all aspects of man should fall within the realm of biology in the broad sense.

old die and the young rise upward in rank. Brains are required for adjustment to these constant changes. Baboons and other monkeys frequently suppress individual drives and desires in favor of group solidarity. Powerful sex drives are held in check during critical periods. Baboons move across the savanna in "battle formation," with the females and young in the center and the males at the front, flanks, and rear. Lions and leopards move aside when baboons approach as a group, but they keep an eye out for stragglers. The biological function of the baboon social group is clearly the defense of its weaker members against predators. Intergroup fighting takes place between subhuman primates, but it does not occur on anything like a human scale.

Baboons and chimpanzees and gorillas emerged from the Pleistocene peacefully — with the brains of baboons and chimpanzees and gorillas. Humans emerged fighting, with brains three times as large. The hands and feet, legs and teeth, of our ancestors became human when their brains were only slightly larger than those of modern chimpanzees. The final change to full manhood was a remarkably rapid increase in the size of the brain. The brain is a social instrument, and the selective force that produced this rapid and complex change must have had something to do with social life.

Oddly enough, this most important of all selective forces has not really been looked for in terms of social life. Some modern authorities seem to think of early men as highly intellectual hermits, sitting alone on the roaring savanna waiting for their brains to develop while monkeys and apes were finding safety in numbers through social cooperation.

A very interesting feature of human evolution is the fact that the force that produced the increase in brain size zeroed in on man alone. Whatever it was, it did not seem to be acting on baboons or chimpanzees. Yet it is often sought among forces that affect other primates as well as men. Weapons are usually assumed to have appeared first in response to the need for food. But how did baboons find food while the men with the least effective brains were starving to death? Even the less efficient human brains were far more complex than those of any baboons. "Something" removed these least efficient humans. What animal drove them into the desert, or killed them outright? More intelligent humans are a likely candidate, but this is almost entirely ignored in recent anthropological literature.

The average size of the brain did, in fact, increase threefold during the Pleistocene, which means that the men with the smallest brains produced fewer offspring, on the average. (Brain size is not a reliable criterion of intelligence when we are comparing two individuals, but a threefold increase in average size clearly indicates an increase in intelligence.) The force that continued to reduce the rate of reproduction of the least intelligent people was an unusually potent one, and it remained potent for more than a million years — even after the least intelligent humans were incomparably *more* intelligent than any other animals.

We cannot actually see evidence of this force in action

during the Pleistocene. We have no films, no tape recordings, no books, or scenes of battle carved in stone. We know our ancestors carried stones that can still be used as meat choppers from China to Spain and from England to the Cape of Good Hope, but we cannot be sure as to how these ugly-looking stones were used. Curious holes in certain early human skulls suggest that human brains were regarded as a culinary delicacy, but we cannot say for sure that the brains eaten were, on the average, slightly smaller than those that directed the eating. Colin McEvedy (1967, p. 16) seems to suspect that this was so, for he says: "If the evidence for man's descent is scanty, we can thank our ancestors, who probably ate most of it."

The dead men of the Pleistocene have told few tales. But one Pleistocene event does seem to be trying to say something. When Cro-Magnon man appeared in western Europe, about 35,000 years ago, Neanderthal man became extinct.

The silence of the prehistoric tomb is broken abruptly at the dawn of history. Wherever men emerged into history, they appeared with a loud clash of arms, fighting for their lives, whether they were in Egypt, Mesopotamia, Anatolia, Greece, Britain, Scandinavia, China, Mexico, Peru, or anywhere else. All civilizations grew in the same way. First there were small-scale battles between small city-states. When one of these had conquered a number of others, and had forced them to stop fighting one another, they were able to cooperate on a scale large enough for building temples and canals and imposing fortifications. Civilizations were thus founded, survived for a while, and were then swept away by bands of warlike barbarians. These illiterate warriors settled on the ruins of the old civilization — and built a bigger and better one on top of it. Then this also was swept away, and so on. One of the greatest of these little city-states of ancient times was called Rome. But even Rome collapsed under pressures that reverberated all across Eurasia from the Great Wall of China to the Straits of Gibraltar.

Human history literally seethes with violent motion. Sumerians, Mitannians, Hebrews, Mycenaeans, Greeks, Parthians, Persians, Scythians, Goths, Huns, Vikings, Englishmen, Aztecs, Incas, Mongolians, Polynesians, Zulus, and many others have expanded violently, brushing other men aside, and killing those that got in their way by the hundreds of millions. Genghis Khan's Mongols alone exterminated untold millions. A force is apparent in human history that is clearly potent enough to eliminate people with an absolutely spine-chilling effectiveness. But was it a *selective* force? Were the winners of wars more intelligent, on the average, than the losers?

We cannot point to any one case and say, for example, that Europeans are more intelligent than American Indians. But we can take a look at some of the requirements for success in war. Wars are not won by sheer blind, brute force in the individual soldiers. The Roman arena showed clearly that individual barbarians could be a match for individual Romans. But a Roman *legion* was no disorganized horde of mere brutes. Roman legions were almost invincible in their day because they were highly disciplined. Their soldiers worked together; they defended each other; they cooperated more effectively than did the bands of feuding barbarians in Britain and Gaul. A single barbarian might kill a single Roman, *if* he could get him alone — just as a lion may easily kill a single baboon — but after trying to cope with Roman *legions* for a while, most barbarians had brains enough to stop fighting each other and obey the commands that crossed hundreds of miles, all the way from Rome.

Cooperation is the secret of success in war, and cooperation requires *brains*. But cooperation is not easy to learn. Rome wasn't built in a day, and armies are not trained overnight. Children have tantrums because cooperation is hard to learn.

The early Hebrews are a good example both of the difficulties involved in learning cooperation, and of the power it confers once it is learned. They were always being warned against graven images, golden calves, and the gods of any *other* tribes; that is, they were warned against breaking up into splinter groups. They were all urged to rally around the same god, and as a reward they were promised the Promised Land.

During the Wilderness period, when Moses was trying to weld the Israelites into a force that could conquer Canaan, they were not the only humans on poor land, looking hungrily down on lands of milk and honey. The entire Greek mainland had been destroyed, every city in Greece had been savagely burned, and the Mycenaeans had been scattered all over the Aegean. "Peoples of the Sea," were trying to break into Egypt, where the Egyptian archers mowed them down by the thousands. The Kassite Empire in Mesopotamia had been overthrown by invading Elamites. The Hittite Empire in Anatolia had been destroyed with a ferocity that melted the very bricks of their capital into a slaggy mass. In China the Shang dynasty was being overthrown by a warlike alliance of tribes from the west. People were in violent motion all over this vast area, and they were not often friendly when they met. The selective premium on intergroup cooperation in those days was sky-high, and untold thousands of ruggedly individualistic little tribes were being swept aside. Most of these casualties were never recorded in the annals of history, but the blackened ruins of cities in Greece and Anatolia and Palestine and Mesopotamia tell a very clear story. The Book of Joshua, chapter 12, lists thirty-one Canaanite "Kings," or cities, that were smitten with the sword during the conquest. The Lord had commanded Joshua to destroy them utterly. In Hebron, "they took it, and smote it with the edge of the sword, and the King thereof, and all the cities thereof, and all the souls that were therein, he left none remaining, according to all that he had done to Eglon."

Sometimes the women and livestock were spared, but the males were always slaughtered wholesale. It is reasonably clear from this that the commandment "Thou shalt not kill" meant "Thou shalt not kill fellow Israelites." It was not necessary in those days to spell this out, as any fool knew it didn't apply to Canaanites. It is also clear that in the commandments, the word *neighbor* is used in a restricted sense. Neighbors were people who belonged to one's own group. Canaanites and other foreigners were not neighbors, and their lives, wives, and land could be taken violently.

Out of this conflagration of bloodshed classical Greece, the empires of Darius and Xerxes, and then Rome, appeared. Civilization had not been destroyed permanently, and when it reappeared it was clear that man's capacity to learn social cooperation had not been reduced. The people who survived to reproduce in the greatest numbers *might* have been those who were able to learn the most effective intergroup cooperation.

One of the arguments most often put forward against the thesis that warfare has trebled the size of the brain runs something like this: The best men are killed in wars, therefore war cannot produce an increase in the highest human qualities through natural selection.

If we narrow our vision to individual men, or to individual battlefields, this argument seems to be valid. But each individual is a part of the group into which he is born. The "best" men are more likely to survive to manhood if they are born into a group that is winning wars. Little Canaanite boys who were slaughtered by Joshua's armies might have grown up to have sons of their own if they had been born into one of the twelve tribes of Israel. While we are young we require protection, and if there is an efficient army between us and the foreigners who would scalp us if they could, we stand a better chance of growing up. If we *do* grow up, we can help our own tribe to increase the frequency of its genes.

Despite their bloody wars, Europeans have increased

their numbers rapidly during the past three hundred years, and they are now breeding on millions of square miles of land that was supporting other races not so very long ago. This increase in Europeans may have *reduced* the efficiency of the brain in mankind as a whole, but when we compare the social cohesion in North America today with that in the same area 360 years ago, it is not easy to prove this. We can be quite certain that the spread of Europeans has produced a genetic change, for when people move they carry their genes with them. Many an American Indian had far more ability to learn social cooperation than have some of the whites who claim to be "supermen" today, but we are dealing here with averages and large samples, not with individuals. There is no race on earth that is unable to make an important contribution to the actual *genetic* improvement of mankind, but it does not follow from this that all men are equal in their ability to learn social cooperation.

Another factor that favors the genes of successful warriors is the age-old practice of polygamy. Nearly all primitive people were polygamous. If the most capable warriors get more wives and produce more children than other men, this could more than overbalance the loss of their bravest comrades in battle. Vikings were outstanding warriors, and Winston Churchill said that one Viking had eight hundred concubines. Powerful men have often behaved in a cavalier way. Complaints were recorded in early Church annals about the behavior of an early Saxon king on his visits to nunneries. Advancing armies have always been liberal with their genes, and this genetic generosity tends to offset the loss of men in battle.

One of the earliest human laws, and a very widespread if not universal one, was the old eye-for-an-eye dictum. The punishment for adultery was meted out by the sword of the wronged husband. This tends to discourage the adulterous plans of unwarlike men, but it favors those of the best swordsmen. Powerful men have always been in a better position to distribute genes, and in human societies, power is usually measured in terms of cooperation. The man with powerful friends doesn't have to rely entirely on the strength of his own two arms. Power comes from cooperation, and cooperation requires brains.

This theory assumes that warfare began more than a million years ago. Many modern authorities reject this assumption. But is it reasonable to assume that birds never migrated before 3000 B.C., merely because we have no eyewitness records? Five thousand years of savage warfare during historical times do not suggest a million years of prehistoric peace. Men have been hanged for murder without having been caught in the act.

The essence of this thesis is that the ability to learn cooperation was actually favored by the selective force of warfare. The "highest" human qualities were demanded by the "lowest" human qualities, with such force and constancy that the size of the brain trebled very rapidly. Cooperation requires communication. Communication is achieved through signs and symbols, and symbolic thought is required for higher mathematics. There was a powerful *biological* reason for loving neighbors: this was the most effective defense against the *hatred* of foreigners. The Golden Rule appears quite naturally under these conditions. As neighbors become more numerous, and the scale of social cooperation expands, the Golden Rule tends to embrace the entire earth. Warfare may thus contain the seeds of its own destruction.

II

SOCIALIZED MONKEYS AND APES

OUR SUBHUMAN ANCESTORS have been dead for a long time. They left a few fragments of bone here and there, but most of these will never be found. Many of those that *are* found will never be recognized as the remains of our own ancestors — and even if we had thousands of complete skeletons in our cupboards, they would not interact socially. We must therefore turn to living monkeys and apes for clues to our social origins. Monkeys and apes are not our ancestors, but they can make us blush with embarrassment as we watch their disarmingly "human" behavior. Certain kinds of behavior are common to all primates, including ourselves — and we can be confident that these general features were present also in our remote ancestors. Since, as we have seen, all monkeys and apes are social animals, we have cause to protest when historians say that human social life began in Mesopotamia only a few thousand years ago — or even when anthropologists tell us our ancestors became social while they were australopithecines. Quite apart from the slur these implications cast on our ances-

21

try, we have no good reason to assume that australopithecines were more backward, socially, than baboons and gorillas and howler monkeys are today. Australopithecines had brains enough to live in social groups, whether or not our own enormous brains have recognized the fact.

MONKEYS

Social life has many advantages, but above all others it provides protection. Baboons move in groups, with the young infants clustered in the center, surrounded by large and formidable males. Groups of baboons have been filmed in the act of driving off lions and cheetahs. A single baboon on his own might be easy meat, but lions think twice before taking on three or four at once. The flesh of baboons is not distasteful to African predators. De Vore and Hall list lions, leopards, cheetahs, hyenas, jackals, wild dogs, and raptorial birds among those who are partial to the flavor of young baboons. They say that in a year's field study it is unlikely that a single predation on baboons will be seen. But such predations *have* been seen, nevertheless — and filmed. The predators look for individuals who have wandered away from their friends and relations. It is not wise for a baboon to be antisocial on the African savanna. In the jungle, monkeys can climb trees and throw fruit at their enemies — but on the open savanna they must deal with lions and leopards face to face. Our own early ancestors lived in the open along with baboons, and they also had very good reasons for moving in social groups.

Before they can function efficiently as a unit, the members of a social group must cooperate. The group must be organized. Individual drives and desires must be sublimated to the interests of group solidarity. Such cooperation, organization, and sublimation are clearly apparent in living primates. When they wish to quench their thirst, individual baboons do not leave their friends; they wait until the group moves as a unit to the water. All baboon groups have a complex "dominance structure" — in the form of an embryonic caste system. The individuals are ranked — not only according to age and sex, but also in more complex ways. A single male "overlord" may be dominant over all the rest, or a "triumvirate" of males may rule jointly, in uneasy alliance. These baboon triumvirates are less complicated than the famous liaison between Caesar, Pompey, and Crassus — and they never have such disturbing and far-reaching results — but there is a deep and fundamental similarity nevertheless. According to W. M. S. Russell's study of Japanese monkeys, the females may choose the male leader of the band. (Social evolution in this species seems to have passed through a suffragette stage.) Russell's article (cited in the References) shows fairly clearly that social classes and political factions were probably functioning long before *Homo sapiens* was born.

The sexual self-restraint of baboons is remarkable. Their sex drives are far from weak; Hall and De Vore report over twenty mountings daily for certain males.

We can assess the power of baboon sex drives — and also their self-restraint under normal conditions — from the terrible results of *human* ignorance. About forty years ago baboons were taken indiscriminately from many different wild groups and thrown together into a large cage at the Regent's Park Zoo in London. There were too few females, and the males had not been given a fair chance to get acquainted. The result was a savage free-for-all fight that went on for days. Many baboons were killed, and the males became so desperately aroused that they killed thirty of the very females they were fighting for — and then tried to copulate with the dead bodies. These conditions were very abnormal and we cannot blame baboons for our own lack of understanding. If a random sample of humans were to be taken from Europe and China and Africa — and then thrown into a Martian cage, with not enough females, and most of them European — the Martians might see some very lively action. This famous Battle of Regent's Park, however, does help us to understand the savage power of the drives that baboons hold in check under normal conditions. In some groups a single overlord may enjoy exclusive rights to certain females while they are in full estrus. Other males, who have been copulating frequently with these females only a day or two before, restrain themselves in favor of the overlord until full estrus has passed. The sexual condition of female baboons is most obvious, even to humans; their genital tissues swell externally to a pronounced maximum, and then recede again toward normal. The overlord claims exclusive rights just before, during, and immediately after the maximal swelling, and it is during this period that ovulation occurs. Therefore, no matter how promiscuous the females may be before and after maximal swelling, the overlord is likely to be the father of the infants they produce. Without causing social unrest through excessive frustration of other males, this remarkable breeding system ensures that the genes of the most socially successful male are well distributed in the next generation. Baboons are intelligent animals, and subordinate males probably trust their paramours not to desert them permanently. This trust, as well as the long, sharp canines of the overlord, probably helps them to restrain themselves. But their restraint is remarkable nevertheless. The old concept of the brutish nature of "savages," who were thought to give way to their elemental urges without regard for the feelings of others, is unfounded. Even monkeys and apes suppress such urges, and our own ancestors have probably been doing so for millions of years. Young men in bands of Australian aborigines show even more restraint than male baboons.

Female baboons also compete for rank, and the winners enjoy the favors of the overlords. Hall and De Vore say that in one South African group the most dominant male rarely mated with the two lowest-ranking females during any stage of sexual swelling, despite repeated invitations from them. These two "lower-class" females had more appeal for younger males. One little male baboon who was only about one and a half years old had his picture taken while he was mounting a low-ranking female. The breeding behavior of baboons clearly favors the genes of socially successful individuals — of either sex.

Social rank in baboon groups is determined very largely by fighting ability. This is demonstrated mainly in threat displays, but some actual fighting does occur — and anyone who has examined the knife-edged canine teeth of a mature male baboon will know that a very brief fight might be very instructive. But social rank is not determined by fighting ability alone. Young males often form alliances, defending one another in disputes with others. These alliances sometimes persist, in the triumvirates of the less autocratically ruled groups. In Russell's Japanese monkeys, a way with the ladies may lead to political success.

Even the most autocratic baboons have learned subservience during their youth. As in the fag system of the English public school, the overlords have all been trained to sublimate their own aggressive drives to the interests of their group — or class — as a whole. High-ranking baboons, like most high-ranking people, know how to threaten effectively — in the interests of "togetherness" — without giving full vent to their potential for ferocity. The smooth and effective functioning of any social group — baboon or human — requires a constant balance between enforced discipline and willing cooperation. The "political" situation is constantly changing as the young grow up and the old become senile. Socially successful individuals must be alert throughout their lives; they must constantly size up other individuals; they must become good judges of character — and this requires *brains*. Without complex brains, the subtle signs of growing weakness in the overlord, or of growing strength in a promising (or threatening) young male, would not be perceived. Even baboons must be able to assess these subtle signs if they are to achieve and maintain rank. If they lacked brains enough for this, they would not be able to survive on the African savanna.

Baboons are clearly capable of unselfish behavior. A large male may fall back when a female with a newborn infant is lagging behind. When the female stops, the big male stops; when she moves on, he moves on. He has no sexual interest in her, and their position in the wake of the group is not the most likely place to find delicacies under stones. No other baboon has forced him to fall back. These big males voluntarily sublimate their own basic urges to the interests of the group as a whole, and in an evolutionary sense the most important of all interests is the protection of the young. The males that fall back to keep an eye on newborn infants, with those who are in the vanguard or on the flanks, are behaving as part of a complex pattern that favors the survival of any or all of the group's more helpless members. All this requires brains.

Protection is the primary advantage of primate social life, but the individuals also help one another to find food (even though they squabble over it); they also satisfy one another's reproductive drives, and give each other emotional satisfaction from relaxed mutual grooming. Most of their lives are spent within sight of their friends and relations. Nearly everything they do is related to these well-known companions. The individual becomes so intimately integrated into his social group that his very existence as a separate entity, sufficient unto himself, is questionable. His personality, his temperament, his belligerence or subservience — almost every facet of his behavior — have been learned .from interactions with other individuals. His behavioral achievements are limited by his genes (no baboon can learn to lead a human army), but the foundations of his personality are formed by the *social* experiences of his youth. This applies to both men and monkeys. When reared in complete isolation from birth, monkeys become abnormal, showing little or no interest in other individuals, including their own offspring.* Our tendency to concentrate on individuals in studies of philosophy, psychology, and evolution may be leading us up blind alleys. We are *social* animals, and our brains are *social* instruments. If we bear this in mind, we may be able to save ourselves from submerging our individuality in the blindness of a social ant heap.

Primate social units hold themselves together. In over fourteen hundred hours of observation of more than twenty-five groups of baboons (by De Vore, Washburn, and others), only two individuals were seen to change groups.† The biological significance of this is fairly obvious. Survival depends on social cooperation between individuals, and it is easier to cooperate effectively with well-known friends than with total strangers. A smooth

* Harlow and Harlow (see References).
† Phyllis Jay (see References).

change from battle formation, with males on the periphery and infants in the center during movements through certain areas, to another formation in another situation can be carried out more efficiently if the individuals know one another very well. This in turn can be achieved only if the *same* individuals stay together. The idiosyncrasies of even *one* baboon (or human) can be very puzzling, and a group of baboons may contain a hundred individuals. A constant departure of close acquaintances, and a steady influx of total strangers, could overtax the learning capacities of baboons. They are very intelligent animals, but even humans take a while to get acquainted. Orchestras, football teams, infantry regiments — and groups of baboons — function better when they have practiced together.

Primates maintain very definite relationships with other groups of the same species. Each band lives in a distinct territory, and although ranges overlap, contacts between bands are relatively rare. They take considerable pains to avoid each other. When two groups meet they regard each other as potential threats. Two groups can use the same water hole without violent intergroup "wars," but usually one of them moves "unconcernedly" away when it sees another approaching. Hall and De Vore described a meeting at a water hole, between two large groups, during which adult males clustered where the groups were closest, showing signs of nervousness. No fighting occurred, but it was clear that neither group had ruled out the possibility of treachery, and both were poised for a violent response if it took place. It is easy to imagine the result if males from either side had tried to steal females from the other.

Primates bark, howl, or whoop, according to mood or species. They are especially noisy in the mornings, and these sounds carry far. The result is a primitive news broadcast. The "international situation" beyond earshot does not concern them, so they have no need for morning newspapers, but their morning broadcast helps them to plan the movements of the coming day in a way that will keep them out of one another's hair. This dawn chorus may be the direct opposite of a "get-together."

Monkeys have dominance hierarchies between groups like those between individuals within groups. In North India, for example, four groups of rhesus monkeys had broadly overlapping ranges. One of these was dominant over the other three everywhere. Of the subordinate groups, one was dominant everywhere over the other two, while each of the two lowest-ranking bands was dominant over the other only in its own "core area." *
This situation is not unlike those days of yore — when Britannia ruled the waves, and men from England wandered at will over the core areas of so many other social groups — including those of Indian rhesus monkeys. The four groups of rhesus monkeys mentioned above were often locked in combat. The dominance of the most powerful group was no figment of the other monkeys' imaginations; many of them carried very tangible scars, and they sometimes limped in remembrance of the teeth

* Southwick, Beg, and Siddiqi (see References).

30

of the most imperialistic group. During eighty-five days of observation, twenty-four major intergroup battles were recorded — in addition to many minor ones. These battles were described as ferocious, often producing serious wounds* — and under such conditions even monkeys have brains enough to learn which group is boss. When a subordinate group saw a more powerful one approaching, it retreated — but if it failed to notice the dominant group's arrival, there was painful trouble. It is clearly important, even for monkeys, to be well informed about the movements of "foreigners." *Human* interest in such movements is so keen that elaborate and expensive Distant Early Warning systems have evolved.

Monkeys and apes seem to be more peaceful than we are, but they still keep an eye out for trouble. Perhaps their greater success at avoiding intergroup violence is due to the greater efficiency of their primitive "morning warning" systems. But even monkeys do not always succeed in avoiding each other, as we have seen — and Sanderson reported "terrific battles, amounting almost to organized warfare — with surprise raids, the taking of prisoners, wide maneuvers, and other grossly human tactics," between hamadryas and geladas baboons in Abyssinia. These conflicts, if they occurred, were not between groups of the same species. But even if the tactics were less "grossly human," they may help to explain why there is only a single species of man alive today.

---

* No fatalities were reported for these particular battles, but in other engagements macaque monkeys have killed macaques, and langurs have killed langurs (see chapter vii).

31

APES

The social life of apes is less well understood than that of baboons and rhesus monkeys. This is not due to a lack of interest in apes, for we are apes ourselves, however naked we may be. Our hairier relatives live in dark forests and jungles where they are not easy to watch. There are obvious reasons for this. Even gorillas are shot, snared, speared, and netted by men — and some are sent thousands of miles from their homes, to be imprisoned for life in cages. Gorillas have good reasons for avoiding human society. Chimpanzees are more cooperative; they perform on roller skates and have "tea parties" for their human exploiters, but even chimps get bored in their cages at times. It is not surprising that most of them hide from us in jungles.

Jane Goodall, and Vernon and Frances Reynolds, have spent years watching chimpanzees in Africa, and they have made many interesting observations. Goodall caught chimps in the act of making tools, apparently unaware that they were exploding the self-definition of man as the only toolmaker. Chimpanzees carry objects for miles. They tear off large branches and wave them at people threateningly. One of them picked up an axe and ran at a human, waving it over his head. He lost heart at the last moment, discarded the axe and ran off again, but he made his point nevertheless: his opinion of humans has now been recorded permanently in the annals of biological science. Goodall's observations have established the fact that a fully erect posture is not required for the use of hand-held weapons. (She saw no signs of jealousy while she watched seven male chimps copulate with the same female, one after the other — which might suggest that chimps are more promiscuous than we are. Certain humans, however, may reserve their judgment on this.)

Two of the conclusions drawn from recent studies of apes are particularly relevant to the present thesis: (1) chimpanzees have no "closed" social groups and (2) apes are peaceful.

Chimpanzee "groups" are described as loose and unstable, with individuals coming and going freely and amicably more or less all the time. This gives the impression that chimps are "innately peaceful," which very neatly fits the belief that humans are (or were) "innately peaceful" also. This is a comforting conclusion, provided we view it very carefully and keep its more disturbing implications out of our minds. If our own ancestors were equally dis-integrated socially, we might, if we can stretch the laws of probability far enough, be justified in hoping for a miraculous return to a "state of nature." The race riots may dissolve into a gay and loving free-for-all, and all our immigration laws may become obsolete. We might all wake up as happy as chimpanzees. But this belief requires a faith that lies beyond the reach of most of us, and viewed from another angle, the alleged absence of segregation in chimpanzees is less comforting. If our ancestors were totally unsegregated, then we have become shockingly degenerate. Chinese and Negroes and Europeans no longer come and go freely and amicably, loosely and unstably, entering each other's homes and marrying each other's daughters without restraint.

The conclusion that there are no "closed" social groups of chimpanzees need not be accepted uncritically. Before we leap to this conclusion we must consider what we mean by a "social group." If our definition of the term is as loose and unstable as chimpanzees are said to be, we will see social groups wherever we look. Four women at a bridge table could be called a social group, as could three baboons engrossed in mutual grooming. A football team could be called a social group, and a gang of boys playing cowboys and Indians could be described as *two* social groups. Among socially primitive humans a social unit may include several hundred individuals, but they will not remain together in a single clump day and night. Parties of men may depart on a hunt or a raid, groups of women may go off to collect food or firewood, groups of children may be temporarily out of their parents' sight. Peaceful interchanges of individuals between these ephemeral aggregations will not provide us with "proof" that social segregation is unknown to *Homo sapiens*. We must draw a distinction between these temporary aggregations and the more stable, larger, social group to which they all belong.

Among baboons and other monkeys that live in the open, the members of *stable* social groups can be seen all at once, and many meetings between two or more of these have been observed. As noted previously, one of

34

the most striking features of these social units is their stability. The same individuals stay together. In fourteen hundred hours of observation of twenty-five groups of baboons, only two individuals changed groups. They also respond as distinct and separate units when they meet, regarding other groups with suspicion, if not with outright hostility. Indian rhesus monkeys fight savage battles — group against group. Among these primates the limits *within* which peaceful comings and goings take place, and the limits *beyond* which they are greatly restricted, are clearly discernible. Among chimpanzees, the fact that such limits have not yet been seen, or recognized, cannot be cited as proof that they don't exist. Among humans, peaceful comings and goings may take place freely within very wide limits, but the limits can be found if we look for them. Peaceful comings and goings take place over the entire surface of both the North and the South Islands of New Zealand, but people of certain races are not allowed to settle permanently in New Zealand. Among humans the *functional* social group (or "political community") can be defined as "that group within which compensation is payable for homicide" * — in other words, the group within which the word *murder* has meaning.† We do not hang our soldiers for killing our enemies in battle. The commandment "Thou shalt not kill" did not apply to Canaanites.

* Mair (see References).
† Carleton Coon (1963) defined a human social group in similar, though less murderous, terms as "a collection of human beings who habitually interact with each other more than they do with outsiders, and form, in a sense, a population."

Subhuman primates are less savage than we are, and so we cannot define the limits of their functional social groups in such bloody terms. But we can find these limits nevertheless, without crippling ourselves in the strait-jacket limitations of an excessively rigid definition. We can set the limits of a *functional* primate social group at a point beyond which the free comings and goings of individuals are more or less clearly restricted. In other words, a primate social group *is* a "closed" social group, *by definition*. If chimpanzees do not form such groups, they belong to a very unusual species of primates. They have either achieved a worldwide Brotherhood of Chimps, or else they are too stupid to draw a distinction between friends and total strangers. Both of these possibilities seem unlikely. Chimpanzees are very intelligent, and like dogs, they probably have brains enough to learn loyalty to friends and to distinguish friends from total strangers. They are at least as intelligent as gibbons, and a sign on a cage in the San Francisco Zoo reads as follows:

"Gibbons associate in family groups and tribes. Within each clan there is little fighting, but let a strange gibbon come near and there will be a battle."

The largest aggregation of chimpanzees seen by the Reynoldses in the Budongo Forest contained about thirty individuals. They suggested that the apparent looseness and instability of chimpanzee groups may have been exaggerated, and that social organization in chimpanzees may not require constant and immediate visual confirmation. Chimps have every right to be offended at the implication that they *may* be this stupid. If they are unable to remember their friends and relations after an absence of hours or days they must be very dim-witted indeed. Dogs can do far better than this. Despite their very cautious suggestion that we may have underrated the social perceptivity of chimps, the Reynoldses, like Jane Goodall, saw a "social group" in every small transient aggregation of individuals. They all agreed that chimpanzee "groups" were constantly changing membership, splitting apart, meeting and joining others, congregating and dispersing. Baboons and humans also do this, *within* a functional social unit. But neither baboons nor humans are as friendly as this with individuals from *other* groups.

Both Jane Goodall and the Reynoldses estimated a total of sixty to eighty chimps in their study areas. Each of these total populations may have been a *functional* social unit, and each one may have been as "closed" as a functional group of baboons — or humans. Groups of this size are not uncommon in baboons, and chimps have larger brains. The Reynoldses' study area was only about twenty-two square miles in area (for example, a square with less than five miles on a side). This should not be unduly large for a single social group of chimpanzees. They reported that "groups" of females with young infants were very quiet, keeping away from the "groups" of noisy feeders — and they suggested that the noisy feeding may have kept these quiet females informed as to the whereabouts of food. They also reported an occasional passage of very noisy "howling mobs" of chimps through the jungle, and suggested cautiously that they may have been escorting females with infants from one area to another, clearing a swath through the leopards by howling as they went. Chimpanzees climb trees, but unlike Tarzan they do not travel far without touching the ground. When they move from one area to another, they travel on terra firma. Full-grown chimps pay slight attention to leopards. Young chimps are very agile in trees. Infant chimps, however, may be vulnerable to leopards while they are being carried on the jungle floor. If so, the Reynoldses' suggestion is a reasonable one — and it implies that all eighty chimps in their study area belonged to the same single functional social group. Such cooperative concern for the safety of infants would have been one of its *primary* biological functions.

Until the composition of an actual functional social unit has been recognized in chimpanzees, and then studied *as such*, interactions between two or more of these cannot be discussed meaningfully. Both Jane Goodall and the Reynoldses say that when two relatively large "groups" meet, or approach one another, the chimps become very noisy and very excited, drumming on plank buttresses of ironwood trees, and so on. Perhaps these were meetings between two separate social units, perhaps not. We still know very little about the intergroup behavior of chimpanzees.

The conclusion that apes are peaceful is based on very good evidence. Humans are also peaceful, most of the time. The chimp who waved an axe at a human had a very jaundiced opinion of mankind — but chimps can be seduced into human society. Jane Goodall received them frequently as guests in her temporary African home. Some chimps live to regret this readiness to place themselves in human hands, when they pine away later in prison, but others seem to enjoy their cigarettes and tea. The vices of civilization can ensnare cats, dogs, cows, horses, and chimpanzees alike. Chimps are certainly peaceful, in this sense, and so was Elsa the Lioness. Both chimps and lions are intelligent and able to *learn*.

George Schaller described gorillas as "rather amiable vegetarians," exploding the popular conception of gorillas as hairy personifications of humanoid violence. He habituated wild gorillas to his presence — that is, he taught them not to fear him. They sometimes approached to within fifteen feet of him, and on one occasion they climbed into the tree in which he was sitting. He was relying on them to keep any capacity for violence they may have possessed under control, and they were relying on him to do the same. But when a gorilla band left his presence, Schaller did not follow them. He said this tended to frighten them, increasing the likelihood of their attacking him. They were amiable vegetarians — provided he refrained from frightening or arousing them. Had he suddenly rushed at them, without warning, from a distance of about thirty feet, the amiability of these vegetarians may have evaporated in a flash. Gorillas are powerful animals with long, sharp canine teeth. A full-grown male may weigh six hundred pounds — and gorillas *have* attacked men. Like lions, dogs, and chimps, they can be tamed — up to a point. But they are not easily tamed. They have been shot, snared, speared, and netted by men for thousands of years, and have become very reserved. They did not accept Schaller as one of them. He did not roll around with them on the ground in affectionate play, as did Jane Goodall with chimpanzees, or as Joy Adamson did with Elsa the Lioness. Schaller was less fortunate than Jane Goodall; he selected for study a far more inhibited species. In the entire eighteen months of his study he saw only two copulations and one invitation to copulate. Although one copulation lasted for fifteen minutes and the other persisted for three hundred thrusts, this was not a large total of sexual activity for eighteen months of patient observation.

Men are peaceful some of the time. Gorillas and chimps and monkeys are peaceful most of the time. But none of these species are peaceful all of the time. They can all be provoked to the point of violence, but all of them keep this potential under control during most of their lives. It is there, however, ready and waiting, even when it is not in use. Schaller says that, now and then, two gorillas ran at each other and slapped one another in passing. He says this was probably redirected aggressiveness, due to his own presence. An aggressive threat from a dominant baboon can send a wave of redirected aggression downward through the entire group, to play havoc with the lowest-ranking individuals. Many people who seem to be mild and submissive at their work return to their homes and redirect their aggressiveness against subordinate members of their own families. Commanding officers send waves of redirected aggression down through the ranks to the privates, who have only the enemy on which to "redirect." We are all peaceful — when others are leaving us alone and letting us have our own way. When we do release our aggressiveness, we try to ensure that it will not bounce back and destroy us.

Hairy apes are more peaceful than naked apes — but naked apes are more often successful in war. Hairy apes have more reason to be peaceful; they are surrounded by men on all sides. In jungles, they can raise their young without constantly presenting an aggressively warlike united front to leopards and lions — and men. Adriaan Kortlandt * has described a form of organized warfare among East African chimpanzees living on open grasslands. A Mohammedan commandment not to eat apes is obeyed by humans in this area, and it is therefore safe for the chimps to come out in the open. These chimps were described as more aggressive and better organized than forest chimps. They were filmed in an organized attack on a dummy leopard, during which they occasionally embraced one another and shook hands. Kortlandt suggests that chimps may have been driven into jungles by early men, and that this may have retarded their rate of evolution in the humanoid direction. This is the direct opposite of the prevailing assumption that our own ancestors were driven out of the jungles by those of the hairy apes. If Kortlandt has guessed correctly, this might also account for the present plight of gorillas, who seem to be even closer than Kalahari Bushmen to the brink of extinction.

Gorillas travel in very small groups today, and Schaller

* See *Time*, April 21, 1967, and *The Observer*, Sept. 24, 1967.

did not describe serious intergroup battles between them. Now and then two small groups met, and sometimes there was a chest-beating display. On one occasion two gorillas from different groups glowered at one another with brow ridges nearly touching, but he saw no fights to the death. Gorillas have large brains; they are intelligent animals who should be capable of more complex social organization than Schaller described. If their ancestors have always been living at such a retarded social level, it is not easy to understand how they acquired such large social instruments (that is, brains). If, on the other hand, their ancestors once lived in the open, contending with other protogorillas, protochimps, and protomen for a place in the sun, it is easy to understand how the less well-organized (less "brainy") ones could have been culled out. They would have had to travel in larger bands in the open. Defense against lions and other primates would have depended on communication, cooperation, and concerted action. When their ancestors became hopelessly outclassed by early humans, the only survivors would have been those who found refuge in the jungles. This is conjecture, of course, but it fits the available evidence.

Hairy apes are not always peaceful. They are able to fight. Rhesus monkeys may engage one another in ferocious intergroup fights (that is, "wars") about twice a week. However, one conclusion has emerged from recent studies which seems clear enough to warrant the rank of a fact: *nonhuman primates do not kill members of their own species by the millions in intergroup wars.* They do not practice headhunting. They do not torture individuals captured from other groups. These habits are very distinctively human.

The human brain, then, must have evolved in response to a greater challenge — and competition with other human brains can become very challenging indeed, and very deadly. Perhaps man should not be defined as the *toolmaker*, but rather as the *warmaker*, of the animal kingdom.

III

HAND-AXE TO H-BOMB

THE MOST PRIMITIVE ANIMALS that can hope to qualify under the term *human* are called australopithecines. These animals had none of the special traits of living apes. They were, as William Howells says, "our kind of animal." They walked upright as we do and the teeth of some species were like ours, even in detail. Howells says there is no escaping it: these early creatures were primitive *men*. They differed from us mainly in their brains, which averaged only about a third of the volume of our brains. They lived about one to three million years ago (the exact date is unknown), and between then and now the human brain has trebled in volume.

Something had been favoring the erect posture for millions of years before these early men were born. That something must have been very advantageous throughout the entire transition from the quadruped to the biped condition, because the biped posture has been evolved despite the fact that we pay for it, to this day, in terms of difficult childbirth, hernias, and potbellies. The selective advantage of semi-upright, and then fully upright, posture was great enough to offset disadvantages involving the reproductive system itself, and in evolutionary terms this means that it must have been very powerful indeed. Such a potent selective force should not be hard to understand, even though we cannot observe the behavior of protohominids directly. Charles Darwin suggested that the upright posture, and also the reduction in canine size, were favored originally because the hands were freed for fighting with weapons. Dart and others have also suggested that survival on the open Pleistocene savanna would not have been possible without an efficient use of weapons. Washburn and Howell and others concede that this may be correct, and Konrad Lorenz suspects that pebble "tools" and other weapons were used by *Australopithecus* to kill, not only game, but also other members of his own species. On the whole, however, modern authorities underemphasize this possibility.

At some time or another the ancestors of men began to kill one another. It is not very likely that this violence began as a general free-for-all. If fights occur within groups of baboons, they almost certainly occurred also within groups of early humans. Australopithecines, with lethal weapons in their hands, may have killed one another occasionally in these family squabbles. They were able to summon up enough ferocity for the deterrence of lions, and if they lost control in a fight they may have committed murder, or manslaughter. On the whole, however, internecine violence must have been kept under control — or else the basic social organization suggested by their large brains would have disintegrated, and

we of today would not have been born. But fighting between separate groups of australopithecines would have
been a different proposition.

Judging from what we know of both men and baboons,
we can assume that australopithecines were well integrated into their own groups, but not well acquainted
with foreigners from other groups. A constant inter-
change of individuals between groups would have over-
strained australopithecine learning abilities. Even today
it is easier to produce an effective fighting division of soldiers if the men are left together in platoons and compa-
nies and regiments long enough to learn how to work
with one another. Transfers and changes are possible, of
course, but military manuals do not recommend a sweeping daily change in the personnel of every unit.

If a fight broke out between two groups of australopithecines, the elaborate mental and emotional balance
of restraints that each individual had *learned* to keep
under control in dealing with the well-known members
of his own group would not have been *learned* in connection with members of the other group. Primates inherit
the genes that produce their brains, but they then have
to use these brains for *learning* the difference between
friend and foe. In dealings with strangers, the full lion-
fighting potential of each individual australopithecine
would have been more likely to escape control. This prin-
ciple is well known: people who enjoy killing and eating
animals are often reluctant to kill and eat an animal they
have learned to know well as a pet; in wars, soldiers are
more reluctant to kill their friends than to kill "enemies"

47

they have never met. Intergroup violence between australopithecines, therefore, was probably bloodier, on the average, than whatever internecine violence took place inside each group.

Human battles disrupt the organization of both armies to a certain extent, but even a routed human army can protect itself from lions. This may not be so in the case of nonhuman primates on open grasslands; when their fighting males have been weakened by intergroup "wars," their infants may become so vulnerable to predators that such groups will be replaced by others with better intergroup self-control.

In the case of early humans the situation may have been different. Women and children alone may have been able to drive off lions, thus releasing the men for hunting trips — or raids. Several dozen australopithecine women and teenagers, armed with sharp sticks or jagged bones, and a powerful hatred for lions, would not have been easy meat. A single individual, even a mature male, may have tempted a hungry lion, but not a small swarm of these weapon-wielding savages. One serious threat to a band of women and children unprotected by their males would have remained, however: an enemy band with a full complement of males. Australopithecines may have lost their immunity from each other when they became relatively immune from predators.

Predation pressure has clearly favored social organization in many primate species, and with each increase in the intelligence of the predators, the social response of the primates must become more effective. But such a contest between different species would probably fail to treble brain size in only *one* of the species involved. One species would either exterminate the other altogether, or else a stalemate would be reached, as it has in the case of lions and baboons. Once an effective counter to a selective force has been evolved, the intensity of the force is reduced and the rate of evolutionary change decreases accordingly. Predation by other species, therefore, cannot account for the very rapid increase in the size of the brain of man and man alone.

What we are seeking here is a force that removed the men with the smallest brains, and continued to do so, even when these smaller-brained men were far more intelligent than any other species on earth. This force must have been very powerful, for it produced a very complex change in a very short time. The human brain contains nine to twelve billion nerve cells,* each with some 25,-000 possible connections with other nerve cells, all arranged in a way that can interpret the symbols of a human language. A threefold increase in the size and complexity of such a remarkable social instrument must have involved nearly every gene in the body, and this colossal genetic change took place in a mere two or three million years. No mild removal of a few individuals here and there can account for this remarkable change. Whatever was hitting the smallest-brained men must have been hitting them hard, and relentlessly, and continu-

---

* Carleton Coon estimates that the number of neurons, in billions, ranged from about 5.0 to 5.5 in australopithecines, 6.8 to 9.4 in *Homo erectus* (Peking man, etc.).

49

ously. Such a powerful force, which zeroed in on man and man alone, should not be hard to find. In seeking it, we must keep the major clues firmly in our minds:

(1) The brain is a social instrument, and therefore the force that trebled its size must have had something to do with social life.

(2) This force was acting on man alone, and we should therefore look for something peculiar to man.

(3) The force was acting against the men with the smallest brains, and it continued to eliminate these men even after their brains were twice as large as those of any other primate.

Predators have already been eliminated as possible candidates. Anthropologists often point out that the need to find food "favored" the most intelligent people. This is obvious, but they do not emphasize that this need must have been so great, and food so hard to get, that men whose brains were twice as large as those of all other primates were unable to cope with the problems of finding food. This seems unlikely, for baboons and chimpanzees continued to find food while men with more than twice their mental capacity starved. The problems of finding food are not peculiar to man alone, and man has always had a very catholic taste in an emergency.

Disease is often considered as a candidate for the force that trebled the size of the human brain. But genetic disease-resistance, so far as we know, is not markedly greater in the most intelligent and socially cooperative people. Disease has certainly played a major role in human evolution, but it favored *disease-resistant* people, and we are looking for something that favored *intelligent* people.

Starvation and disease and accidents have killed many men, but they have also killed many other animals. They have probably favored an increase in famine-resistance, disease-resistance, and agility — in man and other animals alike. But we are looking for something distinctively human, and no other mammals fight wars on anything like a human scale. Man alone does this. Warfare seems to fill all the requirements of the powerful, built-in, distinctively human force we are seeking.

Australopithecines were surely *able* to fight little wars with one another, and the state of affairs in the days when they were the most intelligent animals on earth may have provoked them into actually using their warlike abilities.

Anthropologists often say that prehistoric men were widely dispersed and rarely saw one another. But we have no good reason to assume they were not numerous in certain areas. Wherever game, fruits, fish, water, or other amenities of prehistoric life were plentiful, australopithecines were probably plentiful also. We can surely assume that they did not remain widely and uniformly dispersed when the climate and food were far better in some places than in others.

We can also assume that australopithecines lived in social groups, since their brains were larger than those of modern baboons. These little social groups were probably sprinkled unevenly over the landscape, with clusters here and there, but with none at all on the oceans, the

Arctic ice fields, or in North and South America. They were probably very rare in deserts, and if we could have seen them from a great height as little black spots like grains of pepper against a white background, they probably would have appeared as large, dark splotches on certain game-rich areas, shading gradually away into uninhabited white on all sides — or ending abruptly on seacoasts or lakeshores. Viewed from such a great height, the dark splotches may have conveyed to us an erroneous impression of social cohesion, but a closer inspection would have revealed that each little social group was an entity in itself, well organized internally but well segregated from other neighboring groups. Group size has probably always been limited by the actual learning abilities of the individuals involved. A constant inward and outward flow of foreign strangers would put a severe strain on learning abilities.

Linguistic differences would have added greatly to the mental problems involved in getting acquainted with foreigners, and human languages can change very rapidly. Distinct differences in pronunciation, and even in recently coined words, have already appeared between the inhabitants of Great Britain and those of the United States, Australia, New Zealand, and elsewhere. This has happened despite a common language and literature, radio, television, and motion pictures. Early human groups communicated far less actively than this, and their languages probably changed very rapidly indeed. In modern New Guinea some two and a half million people speak at least seven hundred mutually unintelligible languages (some of which are as different as Chinese and English). Tribes of American Indians and Australian aborigines also spoke many tongues before they began to learn English — or French — or Spanish. The number of different languages that human, or humanoid, brains might devise is about as near to infinity as anything could be, and a fantastic variety of languages must have come and gone during the past two million years. Friendly communication between groups of australopithecines, then, must have been severely inhibited by language difficulties, even if they all had the best of peaceful intentions. A screech that meant "I love you" in one group may have meant "go for your hand-axe!" * in another. Such difficulties could have caused serious misunderstandings, and the learning capacities of australopithecines would have been greatly strained if each of them had to learn several very different protolanguages while he was growing up. Their brains, after all, were scarcely larger than those of modern chimpanzees.

We can assume, then, that the groups were well segregated from one another, even where they were clustered in food-rich areas. Each of these little groups must have been concerned with its own interests. Each one probably regarded its own survival as more important than that of any other group. Any oversympathetic little groups that may have existed, for a while, would have found

* Prehistoric "hand-axes" (stones shaped for hand use) are now called "tools," but they may have been used as weapons; severe head wounds are virtually universal in *Homo erectus* skulls (see Coon, 1963). Spears are good for stabbing hearts, but stones are better for bashing skulls.

themselves starving in deserts or freezing to death in the snows of Kilimanjaro. Where these well-segregated little groups were most numerous they would have found their interests conflicting most often. The grass in the other fellow's yard may have looked as green to them as it does to us. Their brains were small but their stomachs were probably very like ours, and they needed food as much as we do. We can surely assume that they competed for the most desirable areas. This alone, without actual warfare, would have tended to push the more "sympathetic" groups out of their home territories, and if success in these "peaceful" encounters was favored by intelligence, then the most intelligent groups would have maintained themselves longest in places where they could rear the most offspring. This would further increase the population density in these areas (quite apart from the natural tendencies for groups to cluster there). Increased population density would increase the intensity of competition, and so on. If the contesting groups were relatively immune from lions, et cetera, but not from one another, the competition between them may have reached violent intensities. If so, warfare would have taken place. The pace would then have quickened, along with the rate of removal of less successful groups.

If we could have seen these little black-pepper-grain groups not only from a great height but also over a period of time — rather like a time-lapse motion picture in which the motion is greatly speeded up — we would probably have seen a seething, boiling movement of all the little black specks, with waves flowing outward from the dark centers like ripples on water. Pressures from the centers would keep sending these waves outward. Warfare would be most frequent and violent where the collisions were most frequent in the centers of the richest areas. Space would be at a higher premium there, and new groups would be appearing more often to add to the congestion. The sparring and maneuvering and threatening would probably ensure sufficient delays between wars to prevent the entire lot from consuming themselves in their own violence, and allowing them time enough to raise their offspring. Such little population explosions could have produced an outward diffusion of groups. Some little groups would be moving inward to contest the richest ground, but there would not be room enough in the center for all, and the overall flow would be outward, into less desirable territory. Innumerable little wars would be taking place, none of them with anything like the level of organization of modern wars, but inflicting impressive casualties nevertheless. If all the platoons of one of our enormous modern armies should begin fighting each other with intent to kill, even with broken beer bottles, casualties could be considerable. Some little groups would be exterminated entirely. Others would be decimated severely and their surviving females absorbed into the victorious groups. Casualties would be high near the centers, but they would also be high on the peripheries, as wave after wave flowed outward like Huns or Vikings or Mongols. Gradually, previously uninhabited areas would begin to darken with little black specks, as pressures from the centers continued, and as brains became efficient enough to solve the problems of survival on previously uninhabitable land. Australopithecines would be gone, and the heads of their descendants would be noticeably bigger. Eventually, even Bering Strait would be crossed, and the "infection" would spread southward, gradually filling North and South America all the way to Tierra del Fuego. The earth as a whole would darken as the dark blotches spread. As brain efficiency increased, social segregation would gradually decrease, and the centers of the darkest blotches would begin to appear jet black in places, culminating in the cities and nations of Europe and Asia and Africa. At one point, a powerful tidal wave would have swept from Europe and Africa across the Atlantic and over the richest areas of North and South America — almost entirely swamping the "aboriginal" specks and splotches between the Great Lakes and the Rio Grande.

Throughout this process, the groups with the least efficient brains would have had the least efficient social organizations, and hence the least efficient armies. These least "brainy" groups would have been rapidly exterminated or expelled by the better organized groups. On a world scale, brains would tend to be most efficient near the "hot centers," precisely where casualties were highest. This may suggest that such a process would decrease, rather than increase, brain efficiency over the world as a whole. But not all the offspring of the brainier groups would have stayed in the hot centers. Some of them would have decided that the central citadels were too formidable, and would have turned away from them to attack more easily conquered groups in other areas. Rather as water seeks its own level, or electricity follows lines of least resistance, these little groups would also have followed lines of least resistance, on the average. As they swept outward from the hot centers, each successive wave would act rather like a vast genetic vacuum cleaner, wiping out or absorbing all who lacked brains enough to hold their ground. Here and there, groups with better genes and better brains would be wiped out by genetically inferior groups. For all we know, this may have happened when Europeans flooded into North America. On the average, however, those groups with the better brains, better social organizations, and better armies would have prevailed. In the vast scheme of evolution, even the invasion of North America by Europeans is but a minor, individual event. Whichever group may have had the better brains, this one event could neither prove nor disprove the general thesis, any more than a single family of four boys could be cited as proof that this was the most likely ratio of girls to boys in families of four children.

This theory is based on several basic assumptions and if any one of these is unsound, so is the theory. It assumes that warfare — defined as an *intergroup* conflict with intent to kill on both sides — began with australopithecines, if not sooner. It assumes that communication and efficient social organization require brains, that brains are the products of the interactions of sets of genes, and thus that the threefold increase in brain size was a biological event produced by biological forces like brains directing hands in the wielding of clubs or spears or machine guns. It assumes that, on the average, the winners have produced more offspring than the losers of wars, that not all the best men are killed in battle, and that the victorious survivors are very generous with their genes. It assumes also, of course, that good soldiers are not only ferocious killers, but also intelligent men who are willing to risk their lives to protect their families and friends from massacre or starvation or satanic foreign ideas.

I will not attempt to prove this theory in any absolute sense, for I am not so sure that there is any such thing as "absolute proof." Both the theory and the evidence for and against it are presented only as food for thought, as a possible approach to the study of human evolution and human nature which has not yet been fully explored. If the theory is sound, however, it has many far-reaching implications. It implies that there is no sharp line between "good" and "evil," and that cooperation, communication, courage, and love are very closely related indeed to conflict, deception, terror, and hatred. It implies that every increase in the size of the brain was produced by the force of the mixed emotions of love and ferocity. It implies that every step of the long, bloody journey from ape to man increased not only the size of the brain but also its ability to recognize more and more people as friends. It implies that the hand-axe not only killed "them," but also swelled the ranks of "us." Today our brains can understand "us" in terms of social groups as large as 700 million. But the hand-axe has been chipped and polished and fashioned into the hydrogen bomb, and we still aim these bombs at "them." We can still summon up the old ferocities; we even exhort each other to think about the "unthinkable." But our very choice of this word suggests that we stand on the brink of embracing everyone in the "us" that germinated in those millions of tiny bands of brothers who learned to die for the survival of infants whose brains, on the average, were imperceptibly bigger and better than theirs. These implications warrant our best efforts to think — not only about the unthinkable — but also about the reasons for our choice of this word.

IV

POPULATION EXPLOSIONS

WAR IS NOT ONLY A DEADLY BUSINESS, but also a very lively one. It tends to stir up emotions that make people move. Many men have gone to war who would otherwise have been content to stay at home. These movements often act as a chain reaction: people move, collide with one another, and arouse one another. Both war babies and war dead result from these arousals, and these are the basic ingredients of human evolution. Some die, others are born. Genetic changes take place. The chain reaction effects of human wars have reached enormous proportions; we have all heard of the Huns and Genghis Khan. But we have not often considered these war-induced movements of people in terms of evolution, or as factors in the process that trebled the size of our brains.

Men have been pushing each other around since australopithecines learned how to handle lions with one hand and fight little wars with the other. The boiling pattern of movements should have persisted into historic times. It is, in fact, overwhelmingly obvious in the annals of history. Colin McEvedy has prepared maps that show a crude, but admirable, sort of time-lapse motion picture of these colossal movements. Huge arrows reach outward from "hot centers," indicating waves of warlike people on the move. The pattern changes constantly as we turn the pages, and the names of the peoples change also.

From the vast array of available examples, I have selected only a few for review in this chapter: the ancient Near East in very broad and general terms, the Mycenaeans and Greeks in rather more detail, China very briefly, and the American Indians. These examples will be discussed from the point of view of the theory already outlined. Those who remain unconvinced that both historic and prehistoric men had a tendency to push one another around violently may wish to study additional examples. The supply is enormous. When studying these examples, it should be borne in mind that most historians and archaeologists base their interpretations on quite different assumptions (for example, that social life and war did not appear until about eight thousand years ago). It is hoped that the assumptions of neither this nor any other point of view will be swallowed whole, or accepted uncritically.

MESOPOTAMIA

The first written records, apart from lists of articles, tell of warfare. One of these earliest battles of history took place in Mesopotamia, and it illustrates the social pressures in a fairly primitive "hot center." The famous Stele of the Vultures commemorates a victory of King Eannatum of Lagash over the neighboring town of Umma. Gordon Childe estimates the populations of these two towns as 19,000 and 16,000, respectively. Georges Roux thinks Lagash was a bit bigger — between 30,000 and 35,000. The two towns were only about eighteen miles apart. The stele shows war chariots and victorious spearmen in close, phalanxlike formation, marching over enemy bodies that birds had already begun to devour, and scenes of prisoners being led away into captivity. It shows the god of Lagash with a stone mace, bludgeoning helpless Ummian warriors who had been caught in a wide-mesh net. There is no squeamish sensitivity in this ancient record of human social life. The ferocity is portrayed in clear, bold lines on the stele.

The battle is said to have been provoked by a minor boundary dispute, involving only a tiny area. We cannot conclude from this either that the people of Lagash and Umma were merely responding to some "innate" hunger for violence, or that they had been infected by a super-natural "devil" of civilization. Perhaps the general area was overfilled with people, with each tiny city-state defending its own little territory jealously — avoiding violence if possible, but willing to fight, if necessary, for its own little "fatherland." There were probably many little territories, with a small group of people trying to feed and clothe itself in each one. In early Sumer, arable land was probably valued very highly. Each little city-state probably felt encircled by greedy neighbors. Within each little "city," people probably saw themselves as honest, hard-working citizens who simply wanted a little more space in which their children could grow up. If every little social unit had the same benevolent view of itself, and the same malevolent opinion of its neighbors, frictions would be hard to avoid, and they would explode now and then into warfare.

The "little" battle between Lagash and Umma differs from those that raged in France from 1914 to 1918 mainly in the size of the contending units, and in the encouraging fact that modern "steles" do not proudly carve into stone scenes of their own side bludgeoning helpless prisoners with stone maces. The scale of operations has altered, but despite the horrors of modern wars, most modern towns are not constantly threatening others only twenty miles away with savage attacks. Warfare was more personal, much closer to home, five thousand years ago. In even earlier times the battles would have been smaller still, but they were probably even more frequent and personal then. Per capita casualties may have been higher in prehistoric times than they have been during the last few centuries.

Considered in narrow perspective, the battle between these two cities may have decreased the average mental efficiency of the world as a whole, but important genetic changes were also taking place *outside* Mesopotamia. People were moving around, and the savage social pressures near Lagash and Umma were probably sending groups outward in search of more easily conquered land.

If so, pressures would also have been building up outside Mesopotamia — but this is not in itself a population *explosion*, it is merely the process that leads to one.

VERY ANCIENT GREECE

Somewhere around 3800 B.C. a mobile "Dimeni people" invaded Greece. They were probably not very numerous, and they were less homogeneous than the single name applied to them suggests. Emily Vermeule says:

All Europe, the Near East, and Africa were populated by small, varied groups of Neolithic farmers whose powers and particular habits seldom extended beyond some geographical pocket of fertile land. These groups kept pushing, receding from, or bypassing one another; borrowing new ideas, imposing their own systems, or staying dumbly out of touch. By the beginning of the Bronze Age, as it moved jerkily from the Near East to Britain, there are so many layered mixtures of cultural traits that one could scarcely find a family of "pure culture" for three thousand miles in any direction. Certainly in Greece the physical racial types were mixed from the beginning.

She speaks of intervillage "visits, trading parties, and festivals" — not of small, vicious wars like those of modern New Guinea — but these early inhabitants of Greece may not have been any more peaceful than Greeks who lived in the same region three thousand years later. The invaders are described as "less advanced" than their predecessors, but they had the bow, and they built at least one fortification wall five or six rings deep. Ivar Lissner says that two waves of people came from Hungary, the first breaking on Thessaly, the second on the northern Peloponnesus. There is also evidence that invaders came from the Near East, and they may have been arriving from several different hot centers. Vermeule refers to links with Anatolia, with "Europeans," with Balkan parallels ranging from Yugoslavia to southern Russia, and also to Caucasian and Near Eastern links. Andrew Burn speaks of a mingling of broad- and narrow-skulled people at this time. The pots of the different settlements of the invaders differed distinctly, and hostility between the invading groups was probably as great as it had been in Greece before they arrived. Traces of the diversity of these waves of early invaders persisted into classical times, when Greek writers referred to various old languages that were still being spoken.

Towns were built on low hills near the sea during the early centuries of the third millennium B.C., and they left distinct traces of what Vermeule interprets as "overseas trade." This may have resembled the overseas trade between the Vikings and the Christian monks of western Europe during the ninth century A.D. Vermeule says the coastal towns were fortified, "undoubtedly because they were menaced by pirates at sea." They themselves may well have been the very pirates who menaced one another. One of these early towns (Lerna) was surrounded by a defensive wall that passed through four architectural

stages, and was then "burned down violently." After re-
covery from this apparent difference of opinion, a now
famous House of Tiles was built at Lerna. But before any
fortification wall rose around it, the town suffered another savage fire (between 2300 and 2000 B.C.), and Vermeule says "a totally new culture took possession of the
town." She calls these newcomers "marauding destroyers."

There is no "destroying break" between the despoilers
of the House of Tiles and the later Mycenaeans, but Vermeule says there is no evidence that they were themselves "Greeks," and that there is no way to compare
their languages with those of the peoples who lived in
Greece before and after them. Perhaps Greece, at that
time, was like modern New Guinea with its seven hundred mutually unintelligible languages. It may be no
more realistic to look for Periclean Greeks among these
mobs of marauders than it is to look for modern Italians
among Caesar's legionnaires. There were many cultural
changes that may have been due to moving peoples while
the "rise of Mycenae" was under way. It is now fashionable to ignore the possibility of moving peoples, and to
emphasize genetic and cultural continuity between the
invaders of about 2000 B.C. and the Mycenaeans. We like
to trace our lineage far back into the past, and we take
great care to follow lines that please us. We like to ignore
the fact that as we trace our ancestry into the past, our
ancestors increase in numbers. Those who claim descent
from William the Conqueror are probably more or less
equally descended from nearly all fertile people who

lived in England when the Conqueror was rampant. On a larger, racial scale, the same principles apply. The term *Englishman* is probably loosely meaningful, in a genetic sense, as a link between the modern inhabitants of England and those who lived in the area when the illustrious William was exterminating villages and laying the foundations of the British Empire. The term begins to lose genetic meaning when it is applied to people who lived in Britain before the waves on waves of invaders had entered the region. The pre-Celtic peoples of pre-Roman "Brittannia" were not Englishmen, nor were the Celts who invaded and displaced them. Similarly, the people who lived in Greece around 1800 B.C. were not Periclean Greeks.*

Among the welter of archaeological evidence from second millennium Greece, one event deserves particular mention. Soon after 1600 B.C. Greece erupted into a "furious Splendor." This eruption was somehow related to a "Shaft Grave" people. The Shaft Graves displayed an extraordinary splash of weapons. Grave N in circle A at Mycenae, for example, contained three men, two women, and at least 27 swords, 16 sword pommels of ivory and gold, 16 knives, 5 razors, one large "figure eight" shield, and probably other armaments that have since turned to dust. Emily Vermeule says there is no

---

* Sinclair Hood points out that Ventris and Chadwick were not the first to make the Linear B tablets into Greek, and that the conclusion came as a welcome confirmation of well-entrenched views. Hood and others think that Linear B was not Greek, that the Mycenaeans were not Greek, and that the first Greek-speaking people entered Greece around 1200 B.C.

sign of a Shaft Grave town, and hence no stone fortification walls. (The walls of Mycenae were, apparently, built *after* the Shaft Grave period.) Were it not for the embarrassingly tasteless ostentation of the grave ornaments, the absence of fortified towns could be cited as "proof" that these Shaft Grave people were a peaceful folk. (Such evidence has been cited as an indication of peace in early Crete and elsewhere.) The Shaft Gravers seem to have expected a need for defense to follow them into the grave. Were they expecting trouble of some kind? Perhaps they thought they might have to fight for their lives even after they were dead, in some Middle Helladic Valhalla. In life, such people may not have been easily subdued. Vermeule observes that it is "hard to believe that the Shaft Graves represent simply a mild progress from Middle Helladic cists."

We do not know whether or not the Shaft Grave people were newcomers to Greece. If they were, Vermeule says their links would have been with Anatolia and the north. Similar burial customs have been noted in Anatolia, Bulgaria, and "beyond the Black Sea." Lissner suggests that yet another new "race" arrived in Greece around this time, introducing the war chariot, but other authorities may disagree with him.

The "rise of Mycenae" is often pictured as a peaceful period of great prosperity. Alan Samuel describes it in these words: "There is no evidence of Mycenaean domination anywhere. The weapons these men carried brought money, not blood. Prosperity was so great that there was work enough for everyone, and the commerce

was so profitable that foreigners could settle alongside
native populations without danger and without fighting."

If the period was really this peaceful, the predomi-
nance of weapons as articles of trade is very peculiar. It is
not easy to understand how weapons could have brought
so much "money" unless they were being used to achieve
the purpose for which they had been so carefully designed: the shedding of blood. The weapons of the Mycenaeans seem to have been the real thing. American and
other children of today rarely shed each other's blood
with war toys, but their fathers often mean business in
more ways than one when they buy and sell weapons. Is
it realistic to describe the adult Mycenaeans as retarded
children, amassing wealth through the sale of disturbingly realistic-looking war toys? In any case, the weapons
business seems to have boomed as Mycenae rose. Vermeule says the output of weapons increased as the period
advanced toward its climax (when every city in Greece,
with the possible exception of Athens, was savagely destroyed). Arms races may not have been unknown to our
ancestors. Vermeule describes the Shaft Grave era as one
of mobile, highly trained soldiers "everywhere seeking
new stations of power." She goes on to say that when
Mycenaean civilization emerges there are many tribes in
Greece, with different names and probably also with
different dialects. Greek legends tell of foreign princes
who came from the east or south to establish new "kingdoms" in Greece. She notes that the Mycenaeans had
training in new war techniques and that they must have

been "pretty redoubtable" with their battle chariots and long swords. All this suggests that the weapons business may have been booming for very good reasons.

Before their annihilation, the Mycenaean cities were highly militant and very small. Childe says the ramparts of Mycenae itself enclose only eleven acres, and this seems to have been the crowning glory of the whole anarchic "civilization." Lissner says that the citadel of Mycenae was occupied by men as early as 3000 B.C., with the first "Greeks" appearing about 2000 B.C. When these so-called Greeks arrived, Lissner says, the city's golden age began. During this "golden age" massive blocks of stone, so large that the Parthenon builders of later centuries could scarcely believe that ordinary mortals could have placed one on top of the other, were piled up to form Cyclopean fortifications. These people were either anxious to show off their pre-Herculean strength or else they had reason to fear attacks from one another. Lissner shows a map of a tiny area near the Gulf of Argos, covering about fifteen by twenty-five miles, and including such "large fortified towns" as Mycenae, Tiryns, and Argos. The map shows nine towns as black squares of various sizes, and three as open circles. All are within a day's walk from one another, and judging from Lagash and Umma of earlier days, and from Greece of later days, they probably maintained a social independence that led to violent intertown conflicts during the alleged golden age. Childe suggests a similar state of affairs on Crete until about 1500–1400 B.C., when the lord of Knossos seems to have eliminated his competitors. Burn, however, infers that

F

warfare came gently to Crete, as the alleged primitive peace became corrupted with civilized vices. He says that in the late fifteenth century B.C. the Cretans were "growing more warlike, or at least more aware of war."

In the latter half of the second millennium B.C. the palace at Knossos on Crete is said to have fallen during an earthquake. Burn says that when Knossos fell, all coastal settlements were burned and looted at about the same time, after which Mycenaean trade and colonization "burst out . . . as though an impediment had been removed." The Mycenaeans, according to Burn, were "of another race," having been tall and bearded, while the Cretans were clean shaven. The fall of Knossos, and the subsequent diffusion of Mycenaeans, suggest that the Mycenaeans may have ceased fighting one another long enough to take full advantage of the Cretan earthquake. The social pressures behind the Mycenaean "outburst" are not well known, but too many people and too little food were probably involved here, as they were elsewhere in space and time.

The destruction of the Mycenaean civilization has been much discussed, and much disputed. Many volumes have been written on the "Dorian invasion," and many arguments have waxed warm over the authenticity of the Greek legends. V. R. Desborough has carefully examined the archaeological evidence, piece by piece, and he has concluded that Greece was overrun and occupied by "Northwestern peoples." After the first savage destruction of cities around 1200 B.C., there is an embarrassing lack of evidence of actual settlement (recall the apparent nonexistence of a Shaft Grave town), and Desborough suggests that the actual Dorian invasion may have been much later than 1200 B.C. This leaves Greece more or less deserted for a hundred and fifty years, during a period when land values seem to have been very high indeed in nearby regions. This was when Joshua's armies were killing everyone who breathed in city after city of the Promised Land.

George Mylonas considers various explanations of the famous fall of Mycenae. He cites Vermeule's theory of commercial disruption and concludes that: "This explanation, formulated so imaginatively, cannot stand close scrutiny." Vermeule recognized, of course, that a wholesale destruction of Mycenaean cities took place, but she sought the causes in some peculiarly lively form of the 1929 market crash. Mylonas reviews also the Social Revolution theories, which explain the great fall in terms of an ancient form of the Russian Revolution or the recent ghetto riots in America. Mylonas discounts these along with Vermeule's "Wall Street" theory. He himself seems to favor a gradual decline due to internal dissension, followed by a colossal series of blows from waves of invaders.

WHEN A POPULATION EXPLOSION EXPLODES

Our so-called Population Explosion has not exploded
. . . yet. Pressures are building up, as they were inside
Krakatoa and Santorin, but these mountains did not *ex-plode* until their internal pressures blasted them into the
stratosphere. The manufacture of a hydrogen bomb is
not in itself an explosion, although it can certainly lead
to one. In a similar way, the events that preceded the
explosion of 1200 B.C. can be described as a gradual in-crease of pressure, culminating in a blast that hit China
as hard as it hit the Near East. Social cohesion is rather
like the rocks that contain subterranean pressures under
a volcano. Without social cohesion the lava of human
violence pours out unhindered, boiling busily every-where, but nowhere building up force enough for a really
impressive blast. With the advent of social cohesion —
that is, of "empires" — human movements were more
severely restricted. The armies of Egypt, Mesopotamia,
and Hittite Anatolia kept hungry barbarians out, unless
they were willing to pay the price of entry (by helping to
build pyramids, et cetera). As the empires expanded,
the "barbarians" were pushed back, colliding violently
with each other as they retreated. Wherever they struck
an area of relative social cohesion (not necessarily a his-

74

torical empire) the price of land was high, and their movements were restricted again.

During the second millennium B.C. little pockets of social cohesion, in the form of tribes on good land who had brains enough to stop fighting each other whenever an even more foreign enemy appeared, were probably forming from Gibraltar to China. China was no more easily entered than Egypt or Mesopotamia, and the great steppelands of central Asia were peopled by mobile men on horses who welcomed women, slaves, and loot, but not hungry mobs in search of food. The problem of too many people and too little food increased as the social cohesion kept movement and slaughter at minimal levels. While the haves were successful at holding the have-nots at arm's length, there was no really big explosion. Eventually the pressures became too strong for the existing social organizations, and a chain reaction of blood-curdling movements swept over Eurasia from end to end. The population had exploded with force enough to flatten all the walls of civilization, even where they were nearly twenty feet thick.

A comparable general collapse of civilizations had taken place eight hundred years or so *before* 1200 B.C., when Indo-Aryans, Kassites, Mitannians, Hittites, Achaeans, and other peoples emerged into history. About sixteen hundred years *after* 1200 B.C. another vast explosion shattered the Roman Empire.

During the thirteenth century B.C., Roux says, the mass movements of Indo-European peoples in southeast-

ern Europe "escape analysis," and can only be deduced
from their profound repercussions on the entire Near
East. He calls this a "time of confusion." "Prolific and
pugnacious" Illyrians arrived in the Balkans, drove
Thraco-Phrygians into the Hittites in Asia Minor, drove
Dorians, Aeolians and Ionians into the Aegean area. The
"Peoples of the Sea" arrived fighting savagely in Palestine
and at the gates of Egypt. The military force of the barbarians *behind* these People of the Sea can be assessed
from the ferocity of those who fled before them. They
destroyed the Hittite empire utterly and forever. In their
younger days, Hittite armies had been as formidable as
any in the world, but the men who stormed their capital
destroyed every inflammable object they could find. Lissner says the very brickwork of the walls had been fused
by heat into a red slaggy mass. The destroyers seem to
have added fuel to the flames, for the materials in the
building itself could hardly have produced such heat.
Not a house or hut escaped the conflagration. The Hittite citadel had walls seventeen and a half feet thick. Fortresses were expertly fitted into the steep hillsides, and
secret military tunnels had been cut into the rock. For
about five hundred years this citadel had been impregna-
ble, but these invaders destroyed it. Men are not aroused
to such desperate fury for no good reason. Social pressures must have been painful in 1200 B.C. Invaders everywhere were seeking land. Real estate values were high,
and blood was the medium of exchange. Burn tells of
Egyptian records of a battle against a coalition of Libyans
and Sea Raiders in which 6,500 Libyans and 2,500 Sea

Raiders were slaughtered by the Pharaoh's army. He cites also an account of Pharaoh Merenptah, describing the Sea Raiders as hungry men, fighting to fill their bellies daily. Rameses II described migrating people with men and women in heavy, solid-wheeled oxcarts, supported by a fleet of ships crowded with warriors in horned or feathered helmets, carrying round shields, and wearing flexible body armor. The movements were called "raids" and the peoples "raiders," but these were no raids. Raiders do not encumber themselves with women and children in clumsy oxcarts. These were displaced people seeking land, and they were desperate enough to seek it in Egypt, where they fell by the thousands in a hail of Egyptian arrows. Other displaced peoples entered Iran from the north, following ancient invasion routes, to become the Parthians, Medes and Persians of history. Most of the moving peoples of this time were illiterate. We can infer their feelings, emotions, and the desperate nature of their plight only indirectly, from the accounts of their enemies, or from the conflagrations they brought down on the people who held the fertile land that could save them from starvation.

One displaced tribe of this time, however, has left a record of its difficulties. This was the Wilderness period of the twelve Hebrew tribes under Moses. The story of the Exodus, the Wilderness, and the subsequent Conquest of Canaan is unique in its details, but the general pattern was probably followed by hundreds, or thousands, of displaced tribes at the time, and this may have been the pattern of human movement from the earliest

77

times that could be called "human." The twelve tribes of Israel left Egypt, a crowded and beleaguered center of social organization — rather as Abraham before them had left Mesopotamia. They suffered famine and hardships in the Wilderness, as Abraham's band had suffered before them. They struggled to keep an internal cohesion sufficient for survival in a world teeming with desperate people. They succeeded, emerging from the Wilderness to conquer Canaan — and thus to displace or eliminate other peoples.

Many, many tribes must have been wiped out during these trying times. Wherever intergroup cooperation broke down within a group of allied tribes, the small sub-units would have been at the savage mercy of other, larger bands as desperately hungry as they were. Natural selection did not favor splinter groups in the twelfth century B.C. The gradual subsidence of this enormous tidal wave of social pressures may have been due to an actual reduction in human numbers over the entire Middle East. Rivers must have run red with blood. This is what happens when a population explosion *really* explodes. The hungry women may not have been able to replace all the slaughtered bodies with healthy babies. Gradually, human numbers may have returned to a point somewhat nearer to the available food supplies and the current agricultural techniques.

Out of all this carnage and bloodshed, during which the premium on intergroup cooperation was sky-high, a new generation of humans emerged. As always, these survivors differed genetically from earlier generations. All the genes and brains of all the slain could not have been identical with those of the survivors. Could there have been a *biological* improvement in mankind's ability to learn cooperation?

ANCIENT GREECE

The actual history of Greece shows not only the movements but also some of the emotions that churn in a primitive "hot center." The level of social cohesion in ancient Greece can be seen from the size of the social units. Burn says that Athens was the unquestioned capital of Attica at about 1100 B.C., and like other aspects of classical Athens, the size of Attica tends to loom large in modern eyes. For people who take social cohesion over enormous areas for granted, a distinct mental effort is required in order to reduce Attica, and the social achievements of classical Greece, to their actual size. Burn shows a map of Attica and adjacent regions which covers a rectangular area of less than seventy by ninety miles, almost half of which is water. Within this area, Attica occupies about a thousand square miles, with all boundaries less than thirty straight-line miles from Athens. This is the "empire" of which Athens was the capital. It was not very big when compared with previous Hittite, Babylonian or Egyptian empires, or with subsequent Roman or British empires. In population, it was tiny in comparison with modern Tokyo, New York, London or Moscow. It

79

was, however, much larger than most Greek states in 1100 B.C. The social fragmentation in Greece at this time was comparable, in terms of square miles per social unit, to that of modern New Guinea, and large-scale social cohesion in Greece remained unimpressive until Rome imposed her *Pax*. The artistic and architectural achievements of the people who built the Parthenon were magnificent, but their actual social and political achievements were very modest.

Burn says that classical Greece was more minutely fragmented, politically, than even our maps imply. Maps often show boundaries between regions (for example, Attica and Boeotia) but not between the cities inside them. This conveys a false impression of politically integrated "states." Apart from Laconia (under Sparta) and Attica (under Athens), Burn says this was not so. Achaea contained twelve small cities, Phocis contained about thirty, Boeotia fourteen, and so on. The so-called cities would be more aptly described as walled villages, and a population of more than ten thousand was large for one of these. Even in regions where the cities shared common religious traditions and festivals, Burn says, they still fought one another at times. In Arcadia there were both walled cities and highland tribes. A similar social situation probably existed in the Nile valley prior to Menes, and along the Tigris-Euphrates prior to Sargon I. Fortunately, the history of classical Greece is known in considerable detail, and probably with tolerable accuracy. It is often used as a small-scale model for studies of modern international interactions, but it is equally valuable as a more or less life-size model of social interactions inside a primitive hot center.

Burn says that every considerable plain contained one or more fortified "cities." Men emerged from these forts daily to till the fields. Wars broke out from quarrels over borderlands. Burn says the "best people" were those who were well established on good land. As population increased, land was cultivated at increasing distances from the city, until it was no longer convenient to return to the safety of the fortress each night. Outlying villages were then founded — or "budded off." People in the cities gradually lost contact with these outlander groups, and called them *perioikoi,* or "dwellers round about." (Burn says there were also ruder words for them.) The more powerful cities often tried to maintain good relations with surrounding *perioikoi* villages, because they could act as a protective shield against raiders. Occasionally, a group of walled villages formed a league which could discourage, but not always prevent, wars between its members. Here we have embryonic tendencies toward intergroup cooperation. These leagues, however, had an outer perimeter that was often a source of dispute between neighboring "power blocs." This social cohesion was only slightly beyond the level of complete "intergroup independence." (Baboon groups maintain such an independence, with cooperation between groups confined to mutual avoidance, to "armed truce" situations at certain water holes, and so forth. Intergroup cooperation in classical Greece was beyond this level, but only just.) Burn says that the history of Greek interstate relations is largely one of rivalry between groups, of attempts of one group to impose its will on its neighbors. Efficient fortifications made it harder for neighboring cities to reduce one another to starvation through seige, so they were forced toward a state of mutual tolerance. Each city was too poorly organized to be able to keep an army away from its own fields for too long a time. Large armies can undertake extended campaigns in foreign territory only after social cohesion has been achieved over some considerable area of home territory.

In the eighth century B.C., Greece was in a state of "settled," but dynamic and fragmented social balance as described above. Despite the chronic intercity warfare, which was probably confined largely to threat displays, and despite the occasional destruction of one city by another, this was probably similar to a state of more or less maximal peace and stability for a fertile area in prehistoric times.

Natural selection would still be acting under these conditions, favoring intergroup cooperation. The pace would be far slower than during a period of explosive human movement like the twelfth century B.C., but the relative peace and stability would be producing the same kind of pressures that brought on the previous explosion. Population would tend to increase above the density that the land, and the existing agricultural and political techniques, could support. This was clearly happening in Greece during the eighth century B.C.

A marked proliferation and diffusion of Greek social units took place, both to the west and to the east. Colonies were founded in Sicily and southern Italy, along the Dardanelles and around the Black Sea. Parent cities tried to maintain contacts with the colonial cities they had helped to establish, and they were partially successful, but the Greek genius for social fragmentation quickly produced an array of independent city-states, warring with one another as well as with their parent cities, from Sicily to the Caucasus. The Greek migration did not include Egypt, or the part of the Near East that was destined to become the Persian Empire, or those parts of the Mediterranean under Phoenician influence. Where Greek and Phoenician territorial interests coincided, they fought wars (for example, in Sicily). Human movements followed lines of least resistance. Vague, loosely defined territorial boundaries appeared naturally, without forethought, between expanding peoples who were more or less evenly matched. "Persian" pressure was probably felt only indirectly by the expanding Greeks in the eighth century B.C., but it seems to have deflected them into the Black Sea. More primitively organized peoples were being displaced by Greeks, Phoenicians, and other expanding peoples.

Ascending series of small social units within larger ones can be seen clearly at this time. Within Greece, all the cities were in conflict or competition with each other, and yet, small groups of neighboring cities formed precarious leagues in order to dominate, or defend themselves against, others. The cities within a league often fought one another, but they were also able to cooperate in defense against attacks from more distant (that is, more foreign) cities. Despite all their internecine fighting, Greeks as a whole were united enough to prevent deep Phoenician encroachments into their territory.

Greeks and other peoples were increasing in number, moving, diffusing outward from central regions, seeking land. From the smallest social units to the larger tribal, ethnic, or imperial assemblages, social pressures were gradually increasing, moving outward, meeting pressures from other expanding groups, forming boundaries behind which pressures grew — as the force of water grows against a dam. A few centuries later these pressures were to become more violent — when Persian waves over-flowed into Greece, to be checked and repelled at Marathon, Salamis, and Plataea. Not all these pressures and movements were due to overpopulation, of course, but this has probably always been one of the fundamental causes of violent human interactions. If human survival in a desirable area has always required successful defense against human pressures, the urge for one group to dominate others may have very deep biological roots. Wars of conquest have always been regarded as immoral — when the conquerors belonged to the other side. But they are not biologically incomprehensible.

CHINA

The Hwang Ho valley in China is more than four thousand straight-line miles from the Near East, and more than three thousand miles from the Indus valley in northwestern India. The Himalaya Mountains, the Gobi Desert, and other obstacles lie between these areas of emergent civilization. Early human contacts between China and the Near East must have been practically nonexistent. Roux says that even Mesopotamia and Egypt were effectively isolated before 1600 B.C. Europeans have suggested that the Chinese received the idea of civilization from the Near East, through "cultural diffusion"; early Chinese used wheat, millet, and other Western food plants. But in 2000 B.C. one of the most effective barriers to human movement was intergroup hostility, and many hostile tribes reinforced the great geographical barriers between China and the Near East. No barriers restricted human movements *absolutely*, but the two great obstacles sprawling across four thousand miles of central Asia in 2000 B.C. must have prevented a lively exchange of bodies or culture. Even today there are certain restrictions to the flow of people and ideas across this area. Despite the filtration of a few ideas through these formidable barriers, it is only fair to credit the proto-Chinese with the creation of their own civilizations.

The Shang dynasty, with its capital at An Yang, was established around 1750 B.C., when the Hittites were founding their Old Kingdom in Asia Minor. At the height of its power the Shang dynasty may have ruled over about 250,000 square miles, an area some 250 times the size of the Athenian "empire" of later centuries. None of these early "kingdoms" and "empires," however, were as well knit as modern nations, or as peaceful internally. L. Carrington Goodrich says the Shang government had many enemies, with whom it was frequently at war for tribute in the form of slaves and booty, or in self-defense. It collapsed when a powerful people from the west, in *alliance* with other tribes, "beat it into submission, destroyed its capital, and scattered some of its adherents to the south, north and east." * This happened during the era when Joshua was killing the Canaanites, all the cities of Greece were being destroyed, Egyptian arrows were thumping into the Sea Peoples, the bricks of the Hittite capital were being melted, and so on. The explosion was in full blast from Europe to eastern China, and "cultural evolution" was reeling everywhere under a vicious torrent of biological blows.

The conquerors from the west established the Chou dynasty in China. They are said to have been at a lower "cultural" level than the Shang people, but they were good at warfare — and at forming alliances with each other. Carleton Coon says that many kingdoms existed side by side in China during the Chou period, maintaining a loose unity until about 770 B.C., after which friction increased and each feudal lord became more or less independent within his own domain. Then social cohesion grew again as the weaker of these small states were gradually "absorbed" by the stronger. Political unity increased, decreased, and again increased — rather like the beating of an enormous social heart, as men struggled

* *Encyclopedia Americana*, 1950 edition, Vol. 6, pp. 527–541.

with the novel problems of large-scale cooperation —
with warfare playing a dominant role at all times.

As the pulsations of greater and lesser social integration pumped away in China during the Chou era, Coon
says, there was a pushing out of peoples as the Chinese
proper expanded. The Thais moved down to Siam. The
Miao, Yao, and Li peoples clung on as scattered village
populations, subject to the Chinese in southern China
but still speaking old, non-Chinese languages. He also
mentions a people known as "Wu" who lived on the
coast south of the Yangtze River. They wore elaborate
feather headdresses, traveled in seagoing canoes, and col-
lected Chinese heads. Coon says they were disliked by
the Chinese, and suggests that they may have had something to do with the origin and spread of Indonesians,
Melanesians, and Polynesians. Here again we have a pattern of outward diffusion from a hot center. The pressure
was increased when "Huns" * were driven from the great
loop of the Hwang Ho River, and reverberations were
felt later in far-off India and Europe.

The Ch'in kingdom rose in China around 250 B.C. The
previous feudal disunity was abolished, roads were built,
and populations were transferred from one area to another in order to forestall rebellion or to guard and fortify

---

* The epithet *Hun* has been applied not only to recent Germans, but
also to at least four other peoples of obscure origin. It stems from the
Chinese *Hiung-nu*, which seems to have been a general term for warlike
nomads (*Encylopaedia Britannica*, 1950 edition, Vol. 11, p. 916). The
nomads expelled from the Hwang Ho loop were not those who brought
chaos to Europe six hundred years later.

G

87

frontiers. When human populations are moved and intermixed, human genes are moved and intermixed, and the result is biological change of an evolutionary kind. The Ch'in people in China were behaving like Romans, who also built roads and fortifications, abolished disunity, and shifted populations from one area to another. Like the Romans, the Ch'in people extended their frontiers, and gave birth to a concept of social unity over a vast area. This concept has survived, both in Europe and China, through very dark ages of social chaos.

The expulsion of the Huns from the Hwang Ho loop must have been an impressive military achievement, judging from the repercussions it produced on people as far away as India and Europe. It was during the Ch'in period and after the expulsion of the Huns that the Great Wall was erected, more than two hundred years before the Christian Era. This enormous wall is one of the most impressive of all ancient records of man's capacity for large-scale cooperation, and it was built to establish and defend a territorial frontier. Humans have been building fortifications of many kinds for a long time. New Guinea natives, North American Indians, and African tribes built fortifications of wood that have since decayed, leaving no trace. This might convey an illusion of peace to future archaeologists who lack written historical evidence. The Great Wall in China has not decayed. It is still visible, even from the Moon, and its message comes through to us loud and clear. From the earliest times that can be called human, cooperation for defense against other humans has probably had a high survival value. If this is not so, it is hard to understand how the Great Wall of China could ever have been built, or why it could have become necessary.

Like the hydrogen bomb, the Great Wall is a cultural phenomenon, but both are also biological. Both bomb and wall were built by biological bodies with biological brains, hands, and endocrine systems. The Great Wall is as biological as a beaver dam. The beavers that built the best dams produced and reared more offspring than beavers that built ineffectual dams, or none at all. Humans who defended themselves most effectively, with stone or wood or sheer cooperation-for-conflict, produced and reared more offspring than mild, ineffectual people who fled from fertile areas rather than fight for them. Men rarely reasoned why or made reply when they were building walls against their enemies — nor did beavers debate the pros and cons of dam-building. The Great Wall of China was a result of biological evolution, and it had biological results. Huns invaded India and Europe because they couldn't invade China. China's Wall diverted shock waves of genes (in people) that altered the course of human evolution from one end of Eurasia to the other. Attila died some 650 years after the Wall was built, and about six thousand miles west of it. As the Huns moved, other people moved before them. Rome fell before Attila was born. People moved, carrying their genes inside them. The present population of Italy differs *genetically* from that of classical Rome.

When we look for the places of origin of various peoples, we often overlook the fact that the situation is more complex than it appears. Imagine a fertile oasis inhabited by a very pure breed of peaceful poodles. If this area is invaded by bulldogs from the west, huskies from the north, and dalmatians from the east, no matter which breed emerges as dominant there will be very few recognizably pure bulldogs, huskies, poodles or dalmatians within a generation or two. After another generation or two the area may be inhabited by a distinct new breed of "dalmapoobullhusks." We can then look to the north, east, and west without discovering where the dalmapoobullhusks came from — because the very genes that formed them had not been combined before the huskies, dalmatians, and bulldogs arrived. We are up against this kind of a problem when we argue as to whether the Hittites entered Anatolia from the east or the west, or whether the Sumerians came from the north, the east, or the northwest. Biological evolution did not grind to a halt fifty thousand years ago, and therefore none of us can claim a racial purity of such long standing.

AMERICAN INDIANS

Near the end of the Pleistocene, men crossed Bering Strait into North America. The oldest surely dated traces of man in America are only about ten thousand years old, and the subsequent diffusion over both continents was therefore rapid. Carleton Coon says it reached the southern tip of South America by about 5000 B.C. This means that diffusion to the far side of the earth had taken place in about three thousand years. Even if Bering Strait was crossed only once, by a single band of a hundred people, this would have been ample time for both the increase in numbers and the spread over two continents. Coon says that a single, unrepeated migration from Siberia could account for the entire complex array of peoples in the Americas when European settlement began. If all the physical and cultural diversity of American Indians in the year 1600 had evolved in only ten thousand years (about four hundred generations), human evolution may be more rapid than many people now suspect. The rate of evolution depends, of course, on the intensity of the selective forces involved. However many waves of people may have crossed the Strait separately, they must have stopped coming a long time ago. There are no clear ethnic or linguistic links between any particular tribe of American Indians (excluding Eskimos, of course) and any Asiatic tribe. Nearly all American Indians are blood group O, which averages as low as 30 percent in modern Chinese and Japanese. American Indians were all generally mongoloid, but they were all distinctively American as well.

We might ask why a group of Stone Age people would wish to cross Bering Strait in the first place, and why, having passed so many attractive home sites, some of them would settle permanently at Tierra del Fuego. It has been suggested that the earliest immigrants were following herds of game across Bering Strait, while the top two or three hundred feet of the world's oceans were piled up in the form of glaciers, leaving a dry-land connection between Alaska and Siberia. This is a reasonable suggestion, and it is also possible that social pressure of some kind may have encouraged migration, from the initial crossing of Bering Strait to the arrival at Tierra del Fuego. Bands of people would have settled wherever the climate and food supply were adequate, and competition for the most desirable areas would have begun as soon as these areas were reached. According to Oliver La Farge, "If you have rich possessions and stores of food, and if you are surrounded by people who have few possessions and poor food, no matter how much you dislike it you are going to have to fight." As people moved southward into America, certain groups would have acquired rich possessions while neighboring groups were on poor land. These are the frustrating ingredients that lead to war. The early Indians carried no maps showing game concentrations in Carolina, California, Mexico, or Peru. Very many small game-filled pockets were surrounded by poor land, and groups established in one of these pockets were probably challenged by other groups who wished to displace them. Each little pocket would have become a small hot center, and large concentrations of these would have become larger hot centers. Groups that were able to remain in such desirable areas would produce more children and more new groups. Movements from these centers, and intrusions into them, would have been under way throughout the entire three thousand years of diffusion over the two continents.

Hot centers like the Hwang Ho, Tigris-Euphrates,

Indus, and Nile valleys began to appear in Mexico and Peru while Europe was reeling from the explosion that shattered the Roman Empire. Fairly large-scale social organization appeared in Mexico and Peru some three to four thousand years after it had appeared in the Near East and China. This is understandable if the original immigrants, who had failed to hold land in Asia, were slightly less efficient at learning cooperation than were the people who drove them out. When the Spaniards first arrived, both the Inca and the Aztec civilizations were at a level of social cohesion comparable, perhaps, to that of the Old Kingdom of Egypt.

J. Alden Mason says that most groups of American Indians at low levels of culture were hostile to one another. In Peru, the earliest villages were constantly interhostile and occasionally fought small-scale wars. People were distributed in little clusters (villages) along river valleys. Hammer-stones, club-heads, projectile points, spears, and spear-throwers were being made from 850 to 300 B.C. Small groups, showing considerable local variation, persisted until about A.D. 200 with little or no indication of social integration over any considerable area. (A similar social fragmentation existed in Europe, Asia, and Africa in prehistoric times, and it persists today in New Guinea and elsewhere.) Between A.D. 200 and 600, one culture spread north and south along the coast, building what seem to have been large forts at strategic places. Mason says these expanding people made many effigies of warriors carrying weapons.

After A.D. 600 several kingdoms, or "empires," had appeared. Large fortresses and walled cities were built and the kingdoms warred with each other until a small militaristic group (the Incas) appeared late on the scene to establish what Mason calls one of the most extraordinary empires in the world. Strategic transfers of people were carried out by these Inca rulers, but they had no previous knowledge of the reshufflings of populations in the Chinese or Roman empires. These genetic reshufflings produce evolutionary effects whether the people who order or describe them are aware of it or not.

The growth sequence from many small interhostile groups through a series of successively more inclusive social amalgamations, always imposed and maintained by force, has been repeated so many times and in so many widely separated places, by people who had never heard of one another, that it begins to resemble other biological growth sequences. Cultural evolution seems to be basically biological. Given human genes, a wide diversity of habitats, and sufficient time, the genes seem to interact and recombine in a way that produces people who are not only able to cooperate, but actually do so on a large scale.

George Vaillant described a chaotic era in prehistoric Mexico, with groups of people competing and struggling to populate the land. The same growth pattern was followed here as elsewhere, and from it emerged the Aztec "empire." The Aztecs were very fond of human sacrifice, but they preferred prisoners taken in war as sacrificial victims. This must have whetted their appetite for war, which in turn must have set neighboring tribes into violent motion. Vaillant says that Montezuma II once brought twelve thousand war captives from a rebel province for ritual sacrifice. During these religious ceremonies the hearts of the prisoners of war were held aloft while they were still beating. A great spectacle was staged each month, and the demand for enemy warriors must have been steady and high. These ceremonies must have had an effect on gene frequencies in Mexico, and a powerful influence on the movements of humans in surrounding regions. Only rarely do men wish to have their hearts so completely bared. Tribes living near the Aztecs either learned to form defensive alliances or suffered the consequences. Natural selection was in full swing in Mexico when Cortez arrived, to remove the still-beating heart of the entire Aztec empire.

Human sacrifice was very widespread in primitive societies. It was practiced by the Scythians, early Celts, the Druids of pre-Roman Britain, the Vikings, and very many others. In modified forms it was practiced by more advanced peoples, by Semitic tribes who sacrificed defeated enemies to thirsty war gods, by the Romans who thoroughly enjoyed the spectacles in their arenas, and by Londoners who gathered to witness drawings and quarterings, and other such gory events. Human sacrifice was biologically expedient if survival depended absolutely on success in war, or in politics.

Cortez altered the course of biological change in Mexico, but he didn't stop it. Vaillant estimated that in 1962 about 40 percent of the population of Mexico was "pure Indian," 55 percent was of "mixed blood," and only about 5 percent was "entirely non-Indian." This was less cataclysmic than the change north of the Rio Grande, but it was considerable nevertheless. The population of Mexico was *entirely* Indian before Cortez arrived.

The American Indians were far more fragmented into independent social groups than most of us realize today. Clark Wissler estimated that some fifteen hundred mutually unintelligible languages existed in North and South America.* Language seems to have been a very unstable feature of human social evolution, and for this very reason it is a reliable criterion for estimating the rate of flow of ideas. Even with all our modern facilities (books, newspapers, television), traditional ideas and mythologies do not flow through different cultures with complete freedom. With universal illiteracy and language barriers on all sides of each small group or tribe, the flow of ideas must have been reduced to a tiny trickle. Weapons technology seems to diffuse fairly rapidly, even through such a fragmented array of groups. Most American Indians had bows when the Europeans arrived. The first hint of an Indian's presence was often conveyed by an arrow. But pottery and building techniques had not diffused far from Mexico and Peru. Purely cultural evolution, therefore, can scarcely account for the more basic similarities in social behavior between the widely separated groups and tribes of American Indians.

According to Wissler, the term *tribe* is loose and unsatisfactory as applied to most pre-Columbian American

* *Encyclopedia Americana,* 1950 edition, Vol. 15, pp. 44–60.

Indians. People accustomed to life in large modern nations tend to think of a "primitive tribe" as a large group of people, dispersed over a considerable area, speaking a common language, sharing a common culture, and cooperating with one another rather as the citizens of a modern nation do. Actually, primitive tribes were not this well integrated. Among American Indians, and other culturally primitive people, the community or village was an independent political unit, "jealous of its own freedom of action and tolerating a minimum of alien control, if any." The groups varied in size according to the way of life, and among hunting peoples they rarely exceeded three hundred individuals. When they became too large they divided or starved. When they became too small (Wissler says fifty or less) they either joined some other group (accepting its terms, of course), or perished (possibly under the blows of another group). Even with agriculture, a town of five thousand persons was not possible without a relatively far-flung political organization.

As groups "budded off," languages remained similar for a time, but gradually diverged. Language affinities over large areas indicated expanding groups — and they were clearly geographical. The rate of linguistic divergence among illiterate people without books or roads must have been more rapid than the geographical divergence of the English language since the year 1600. Linguistic affinities over a large area probably indicated expansion during a few centuries. Not all groups could have been expanding, and the language families suggest that some had been doing so at the expense of others. We

97

know this was taking place in Mexico and Peru, and linguistic evidence suggests that it was general over both continents.

Viewed from an Olympian perspective in space and time, human movement (that is, gene flow) would probably have appeared as a series of smaller and larger explosions, sending ripples outward in all directions. Most of the waves would come from fertile pockets or hot centers. The diffusions from one center would tend to block those from others. Successive diffusions would increase social pressures within each territory and the more powerful of these would overcome the weaker, to flow farther afield along lines of least resistance. Groups in these lines of least resistance were probably exterminated, or severely decimated before they were assimilated.

The actual mechanism of such a diffusion can be seen in the advance of Europeans through America. Wissler says the Europeans encouraged intervillage feuds, and thus used the Indians as the agents of their own destruction. This ancient rule — divide and conquer — has probably had a high survival value since intergroup cooperation first appeared. But the word *divide* must always apply to the enemy. The Europeans were also disunited, but far less so than the Indians. The English, French, Spanish, and Portuguese were all cooperating with their own respective groups, even across the ocean. Competition between these evenly matched groups in Europe was producing the social pressure that sent them diffusing outward, along lines of least resistance, into America, Africa, Asia, and Australia.

Language families provide indirect evidence of human movements in early America, but there is also archaeological evidence of an advance of powerful tribes up the Mississippi and Ohio rivers. Among these were the famous Cherokees and Iroquois, who had apparently displaced, absorbed, or exterminated an array of earlier cultures. Tribes La Farge calls "friendly coastal Indians" had been crowded against the sea. The actual pressures that forced the friendly coastal tribes to retreat are well known. They were felt by both the French and the English. The Cherokees and Iroquois fought wars with a religious fervor. La Farge says that when the British urged one group of Cherokees to make peace with another, the Indians explained that unless they were at war with *some* tribe, "they would not know what to do with themselves." They considered warfare as "the greatest of delights." La Farge says they tried not to spoil a war by winning it, or to subjugate or drive other tribes from their territory. This may have been so if their territory was overloaded with game and other food, but it seems unlikely that they would have tolerated poaching when game was scarce. However much they may have wished to discourage the tribes with whom they shared the delights of war from evacuating, some of them evacuated anyway. The friendly coastal Indians were as far away from the Cherokees and Iroquois as they could get, without seagoing canoes.

Life within reach of the Cherokees could become unpleasant. They had bows, but they preferred close combat with spears and clubs. They took legs and arms, but preferred scalps, or entire heads. La Farge says the killing of women and children was highly esteemed, since a leg, arm, scalp or head from one of these was proof that the warrior had penetrated to the very heart of the enemy village. Male prisoners were not easily taken alive, in good condition, since death was often preferred to participation in the religious devotions of an enemy village. Healthy male prisoners delighted the inhabitants of a victorious village, for they could then be tortured elaborately by the women. The Iroquois also tortured their prisoners, using females when males were not available. La Farge quotes a prayer to their god of war and hunting: "We offer thee this victim which we burn for thee, that thou mayest be filled with her flesh and render us ever anew victorious over our enemies."

Victims were sometimes kept alive for as long as twenty-four hours, fed between agonies to keep up their strength, loved and admired — and perhaps eaten — if they showed enough courage. La Farge says that on one occasion young men and women were rebuked for running off together into the woods during the ceremony, which showed a lack of respect "for the man who was so bravely entertaining everyone." The entertainment seems to have provided physical as well as spiritual pleasures. Sometimes endearing terms were addressed to the victim as the glowing brands were gently applied to very painful spots.

The flight of the friendly coastal tribes before these people is understandable, but it was not a good formula for survival. Their days were probably numbered, for their lands were teeming with game and the Cherokees and Iroquois were enthusiastic hunters. In any case, they received a swift coup de grace from the Europeans. La Farge says they received the French and English in friendship. When Powhatan was about to decapitate John Smith, the chief's daughter Pocahontas is said to have saved John's neck by placing her own upon it. This very friendly act was futile, however, for Powhatan attacked the British soon afterward. He had every reason to attack them, for they were following lines of least resistance into his land, but he received a swift lesson in British justice. Had he fled westward he would have run head-on into Cherokee justice. He was caught in the jaws of the primeval human nutcracker, and he was not alone in this predicament. In Massachusetts, Rhode Island, Connecticut, and New York the Indians either resisted the diffusing English and Dutch, or submitted peacefully to what La Farge describes as massacre after massacre, in which hundreds of Indian women and children were slaughtered or burned alive. The Narragansets and the Pequots were exterminated, and only a handful of Mohicans still survive in Connecticut. The Mugwumps tried to remain neutral, but are now extinct. La Farge says that at one time eighty severed Indian heads were displayed on the streets of seventeenth-century Manhattan, where the wife of the Dutch governor is said to have played football with them.

The elimination of the friendly coastal tribes was a biological event. Not even *human* death can be purely cultural. The social achievements of the Cherokees and

Iroquois were also biological — for they were accomplished through physical interactions within and between human brains. The brains of Iroquois, Aztecs, and Incas arrived independently at the same general approach to the problem of large-scale cooperation. They discovered the answer to this problem without help from men who had died thousands of years before their time in China, Egypt, and Rome. Douglas Leechman describes what may have been a universal first step toward civilization in these words: "The chief purpose of the League of the Iroquois was to stop the fighting among the tribes and bring about universal peace, and they fought like demons to attain this goal. It sounds like a most contradictory way of going at it, but at times the best way to make somebody stop fighting is to fight him till he does stop."

This was the formula of Menes of Egypt, the *Pax Romana*, the *Pax Britannica*, and of every other society that suppressed intervillage feuds efficiently enough to found a civilization.

V

HAREMS AND NATURAL
SELECTION

CHARLES DARWIN was aware of the possibility that wars may have had an evolutionary effect, but he was unable to explain this in terms of his rather restricted conception of natural selection. In his *Descent of Man* he said:

Let it be borne in mind how all-important, in the never-ceasing wars of savages, fidelity and courage must be. The advantage which disciplined soldiers have over undisciplined hordes follows chiefly from the confidence which each man feels in his comrades. . . . A tribe rich in the above qualities would spread and be victorious over other tribes: but in the course of time it would, judging from all past history, be in its turn overcome by some other tribe still more highly endowed. Thus the social and moral qualities would tend slowly to advance and be diffused throughout the world.

This is natural selection on a grand scale, but Darwin was thinking in narrower terms. In his next paragraph he said:

But it may be asked, how within the limits of the same tribe did a large number of members first become endowed with these social and moral qualities, and how was the standard of excellence raised. It is extremely doubtful whether the offspring of the more sympathetic and benevolent parents, or of those who were the most faithful to their comrades, would be reared in greater numbers than the children of selfish and treacherous parents belonging to the same tribe. He who was ready to sacrifice his life, as many a savage has been, rather than betray his comrades, would often leave no offspring to inherit his noble nature. The bravest men, who were always willing to come to the front in war, and who freely risked their lives for others, would on an average perish in larger numbers than other men. Therefore it hardly seems probable, that the number of men gifted with such virtues, or that the standard of their excellence, could be increased through natural selection, that is, by the survival of the fittest; for we are not here speaking of one tribe being victorious over another.

It is ironic that Darwin, who spent much of his life trying to explain human evolution in terms of natural selection, provided his opponents with this seemingly insurmountable barrier. This reasoning has been used for nearly a hundred years to keep biology and evolution away from the altars of human nature.

Darwin saw the recurrent diffusions of ever more "highly endowed" tribes as a possible explanation of the evolution of our most distinctively human characteristics. He saw brave warriors as "noble," "sympathetic," and "benevolent" people — and he saw those who held back from the fray as "selfish and treacherous." Had he

seen a greater reproductive potential in these noble warriors he would surely have applied his theory of natural
selection to the evolution of our highest human qualities.
But he was confining his attention too closely "within
the limits of the same tribe," and he overlooked the fact
that males can father many offspring. Darwin's belief
that selfish and treacherous people rear the most offspring need not be accepted uncritically. Selfish mothers
often neglect or abandon even those offspring they might
accidentally produce. His choice of adjectives was unfortunate also, and has led to much confusion. We are all a
little selfish and treacherous at times; even some of the
world's greatest and bravest warriors have been accused of
these vices (especially by their defeated enemies). We
are all paradoxical mixtures of tenderness and ferocity,
generosity and selfishness. We turn these aspects of our
natures on and off according to circumstances, and we are
all a bit concerned with the way the wind is blowing at
any particular moment. Success in war does not depend
entirely on the sympathy and benevolence of the "noblest" warriors. The talents of cutthroats can be used
very effectively during wars. All good soldiers are killers,
but they also submit to discipline, and they often risk
their lives with almost incredible courage. Success in war
is determined by many things, but it depends above all
on social cooperation. Whatever the morality of such cooperation may be, it demands intelligence and very complex brains. Caesar could not have conquered Gaul with
an army of australopithecines. The problem before us is
whether or not the most effective warriors produce the

most offspring. Whether these warriors were selfish or generous, faithful or treacherous, is beside the point. We can take it for granted that enemy warriors are often very selfish and treacherous, while our own boys are usually noble and self-sacrificing. But we are dealing with the problem of whether warfare could have increased the size and efficiency of our brains, and as we do this we must try to refrain from calling each other names.

Most of the many factors that favor the reproductive potential of cooperative people and good warriors can be grouped under two categories: (1) the genetic effects of increased *Lebensraum* and (2) the genetic effects of polygamy.

LEBENSRAUM

The effects of increased *Lebensraum* seemed fairly obvious, even to Darwin. If the ability to learn cooperative behavior is inherited, if both individuals and tribes differ in these inherited abilities, and if the most cooperative and disciplined tribes push the "undisciplined hordes" off the best land, then it follows that the genes of the winners will become more numerous and widespread. As Darwin put it, the social and moral qualities would advance and be diffused through the world. When he viewed the problem in these broad terms, he saw no great difficulties. He became puzzled only when he looked more closely at a single tribe and saw the noblest warriors falling while the laggards lived on.

Only one example from the vast array of those available need be mentioned here. Europeans are descended from a long line of warlike ancestors. These ancestors have slaughtered each other by the hundreds of millions during the past few thousand years, and if warfare tends to cull out those who risk their lives, the survivors of all this carnage should now be less warlike and more cautious. Instead, they have produced more nuclear weapons than all the non-Europeans put together, and they are now aiming these weapons at one another. The production of nuclear weapons requires both intelligence and cooperation, and however unintelligent it may be to aim such things at one another, doing so clearly indicates a readiness to risk life and limb. During the past three centuries the number of Europeans on the earth has increased about twelvefold, while the number of Asians has increased only fivefold.* Europeans (in the broad sense) are now rearing their children in Australia, New Zealand, South Africa, North America, South America, and across northern Asia to the Pacific — and Europe itself contains more Europeans than ever before. The failure of some of them to conquer and hold *Lebensraum* has not prevented other Europeans from doing so. Despite their wars, or perhaps because of them, these people have increased their numbers more rapidly than any other people on earth. As they did so, they often thought in

* Lasker (see References).

terms of a "yellow peril," and many of them still think in
these terms. Non-Europeans, however, have had good
cause to think in terms of a "white peril," especially the
Africans who sailed to North America on slave ships. Not
only have the Europeans increased their own numbers
(thereby increasing the frequency of their genes), they
have also *decreased* the numbers of certain peoples who
stood in their path. They exterminated the old Tasmanians altogether, reduced the Australian aborigines to
about fifty thousand "fullbloods," and drastically reduced the numbers of many North American Indians. In
the region between Canada and Mexico the frequency of
North American Indian genes in the year 1600 was one
hundred percent. Today, only twelve generations later, it
is only about a quarter of one percent.* Europeans have
also mingled their genes with those of many other
peoples. Many Mexicans and South Americans and
American Negroes and others now carry genes inherited
from European ancestors. These are the genetic and evolutionary effects of increased *Lebensraum*. Advancing
armies have always been very generous with their genes.
Whether the genetic potential of *Homo sapiens* for producing brains that can learn social cooperation has been
increased or decreased by this explosive increase in Europeans, the fact remains that social cooperation is far
more advanced and complex today than it was in the year
1600.

According to Darwin's theory of natural selection, individuals who are best able to cope with the environment

* La Farge, 1960 (see References).

around them will produce the most offspring, on the average. In the case of humans and baboons the social group into which the individual is born is the most important feature of the environment around it. If a child is unable to integrate into his group, his reproductive potential will be low. A young man who is growing up in a war-winning group may be in a better position to mingle his genes with those of the captive women who are coming in with the rest of the loot, especially if he happens to be the favorite son of the group's greatest warrior.

POLYGAMY

Polygamy occurs in two forms. In polyandry, a single wife has more than one husband. In polygyny, a husband has more than one wife. Polyandry is known in humans, but polygyny is far more common. Unless otherwise specified, the term *polygamy* is usually assumed to mean the more common practice. Bronislaw Malinowski says there are very few primitive tribes in which a man is not allowed, if he can, to have more than one wife.* We must remember that not all of the men of a group can have more than one wife — unless that group has been very successful in the capture of "enemy" women. The sex ratio is roughly fifty-fifty in all human groups. If the males are decimated by war casualties until there are two

* *Encyclopaedia Britannica,* 1950 edition, Vol. 14, p. 949.

wives apiece for the survivors, it is likely that the men will be slaves and the women concubines of the conquerors.

If in a certain small group one man has ten wives and the other nine men have none, we can be fairly confident that the much-married man is no weakling. Large harems have usually been the prerogative of chiefs and kings. African chiefs seem to have had a particular taste for variety. King Mtessa of Uganda, for example, is said to have had about seven thousand wives. This seems to have been a record. If he cohabited with each wife once a year he would have been dealing with about nineteen each day. Unless his tribe had captured enemy women in recent wars, some seven thousand of his male subjects must have had no wives at all. This would have caused unrest, so we can probably assume that Mtessa's tribe was successful in war, and thus that he himself was an efficient war leader — whether he preceded his men into battle or not. If so, this efficient war leader may have been distributing more genes than anyone else in his tribe. His best warriors would not have been risking their lives without *some* share in the loot, so his tribe as a whole was probably producing more offspring than were the tribes that supplied the women. One man can father more offspring in one year than a dozen women can produce in ten. Prize bulls are more expensive than cows. Males have a far more potent effect on evolution. Not all the best warriors will be killed when their side is victorious, and some of them will readily take over the genetic tasks of their fallen comrades.

Men who make an inadequate contribution to the defense of the tribe are often discouraged from making a genetic contribution. Peter Matthiessen, who described the observations of the recent Harvard-Peabody expedition to New Guinea (during which Michael Rockefeller lost his life), says that not all men are equally cooperative warriors in the Kurelu tribe. Some of them go to war with the others, but remain well to the rear. During lulls in the battle they are allowed to associate with, or even to sit beside, the greatest warriors. They are nevertheless held in some contempt, and their rank in the dominance structure of the group is low. They are called "kepu," which means "a-man-who-has-not-killed." According to Matthiessen they are never jeered or driven into battle, but any wives or pigs they have might be taken from them. Few kepu men have more than one wife, and many have no wives at all. Matthiessen says that the wife of a kepu man, if he has one, might be raped by other men. This, he says, is the law, and should the kepu man resist it he might be killed or expelled from the group. The great "kains," or war leaders, have more than one wife. A man's status is measured in terms of wives and pigs. Matthiessen describes one Kurelu kain who had four wives and eleven pigs, which made him a rich man. This man was ambitious, had a "rare gift for intrigue," and was either a good warrior or succeeded in convincing others that he was. Under these conditions, young men were as expendable as young male baboons, and they had to wait their turn for wives. Matthiessen quoted a song that young Kurelu men sing:

Where have all the young girls gone?
We danced with them at the Liberek
And now they are all married.
Well, what can be done,
When the kains take all the women?

The answer was obvious: become a kain. Toying with
the affections of the wives of kains was dangerous. Matthiessen says the kains were eager to kill such philander-
ers; this was one of the privileges of kainship. Young
Kurelu men might be able to "use" the wife of a kepu
man, but if they wanted wives of their own the road toward them passed through the battlefield.

Other recent studies of primitive peoples show that an
unequal distribution of female wealth is often a source of
violence. In a book about Australian aborigines, I. L.
Idriess described the results of a fight to the death between two men, one of whom had stolen the wife of the
other, who belonged to another tribe. One of the dead
men had a spear in his back, but his teeth were locked in
the badly gnawed throat of his enemy. This was not warfare in the modern sense, but it suggests one of the
sources from which modern warfare may have evolved.
The two men belonged to different tribes. Both tribes
practiced polygamy, denying wives to their young men
unless they could be stolen from neighboring groups.
The old men held much power, and had more than their
fair share of wives. The young men were thereby deprived of women but not of spears. They were expected
to devote themselves to becoming good warriors, for the

survival of the tribe. They would be allowed to marry when they had proved their manhood through a kill in vendetta or war. Woman-raiding on a hostile tribe was acceptable, but they were warned that if ever they stole a tribal girl who had already been allotted by the elders, they would be killed. Idriess says the young men believed this as surely as they believed the sun would set. Woman-raiding led to blood feuds. Warfare with large armies was unknown to the early aborigines, but they were not as mild as we are sometimes led to believe. Even Elliot Smith, a passionate advocate of the doctrine that man is peaceful by nature, referred to intertribal feuds in Australia, some of which he said were "constant."

Unequal distributions of wealth promote frictions between the haves and the have-nots. With the high premium on women in polygamous societies it is obvious that adultery will not be dismissed lightly. Even in periods noted for moral laxity, and in ostensibly monogamous societies, adultery can cause a politician to lose an election. In primitive societies, punishments can be more severe.

Among the Nuer tribesmen of Africa the appropriate reaction to adultery is for the cuckolded husband to challenge the male adulterer to single combat. If the dispute is within a village, clubs are used rather than the deadly Nuer spears. Honor prevents a man from giving in until he is too badly injured to continue, but other villagers may do what they can to prevent fatalities. Cuckolded husbands were probably punished severely for the infidelity of their wives, by powerful adulterers who enjoyed demonstrating the full force of their blows to the assembled villagers. Under such conditions, timid husbands probably find it easier to learn tolerance for the peccadilloes of their wives.

When Abraham entered Egypt, he introduced his wife Sarah as his sister, because he feared that powerful Egyptians would kill him in order to have her if he admitted that she was his wife. Later on, Isaac introduced his wife Rebecca as *his* sister, when he sought help from Abimelech during another famine. The fact that these incidents were recorded in the Old Testament suggests that small tribes seeking food from larger ones expected cavalier treatment from the ruling aristocracies. The morality of these virtual offers of wives to powerful foreigners may not be highly regarded by modern men, but social conditions were different three thousand years ago. Small tribes probably avoided more powerful tribes unless they were on the brink of starvation, or in flight from even more barbaric enemies. The virtues of early Hebrew women were not regarded lightly by their men. For example, Dinah, the sister of Simeon and Levi, was taken by Shechem the Hivite, whose intentions were honorable. Shechem asked for Dinah's hand in marriage. In reply, Simeon and Levi massacred all Hivite males and took all their women, children, sheep, oxen, asses, and other wealth. Genetic exchanges between tribes were apparently sought avidly on the one hand and resisted violently on the other.

Polygamy was practiced by the Hebrews, early Egyptians, Africans, American Indians, ancient Britons and

Irish, early Greeks, Slavs, Teutons, Ottoman Turks, Hindus, Chinese, early Japanese, New Zealand Maoris, New Guinea tribes, early Franks, early kings of France, including Charlemagne and other Christians, early Christian priests, and so on down to Frederick Wilhelm II of Prussia. This is only a partial list, and it includes only peoples who sanctioned several *wives*, if the men were strong enough to get and keep them. It does not include concubinage, which has the same evolutionary effects as marriage, nor does it include the cavalier behavior of powerful men. If we can assume that australopithecines were no more monogamous than all the peoples listed above, there must have been not only a powerful evolutionary bias towards the genes of warriors, but also a powerful motive force promoting intergroup violence throughout the entire history and prehistory of mankind. With all due respect to the women, territory has probably always been the major source of war, but women have also been worth the risk of life and limb in the eyes of men for a long time. In the course of discussions at a recent symposium in London,* J. B. S. Haldane agreed with the Reverend H. C. Trowell that the human race has been polygamous for the best part of a million years, and that under polygamy "the favored and cultured person, the king or chief, sires a large number of people in the community, and under those conditions we ought to have intelligence building up more rapidly than under the conditions of monogamy." This view was not disputed by the impressive array of leading thinkers present.

* Reported in G. Wolstenholme, p. 292 (see References).

It seems to be fairly clear that, whether we like it or not, polygamy may have helped to treble the size of our brains.

MUTATION

Mutation provides the raw material, but it does not determine the *course* of evolution. This is determined by natural selection. Mutation increases the variety of the genes available, and natural selection removes those that fail to interact in such a way as to produce a well-coordinated living organism. Living organisms are so exquisitely coordinated that even a single uncooperative gene can disrupt the entire system. Mutations that produce such genes are called "lethals." Even if the mutated gene does not kill the organism outright, it will nearly always have harmful effects. Any random change in a complex mechanism is likely to reduce its efficiency. A rifle bullet fired at a swiftly moving automobile might conceivably improve the carburetor adjustment, and an atomic "bullet" is about as likely to improve the coordination of a living organism.

The human population of today is rather like a large convoy of vehicles passing through a hostile area in which an occasional rifle is fired toward it. Here and there a vehicle is stopped by a bullet, but the convoy as a whole keeps moving. An increase in the rate of mutation would be like an increase in the volume of hostile fire against the convoy. The aftereffects of a nuclear war, in some areas, would be rather like a very heavy attack from strafing aircraft, with an enormous increase in the volume of fire from the roadside. Such an attack would produce more harmful than beneficial carburetor "adjustments." Like all analogies, this one breaks down when carried too far. Automobiles do not reproduce themselves, and damage from small-arms fire would not be replicated and recombined in future "generations" of vehicles. Even if vehicles *did* reproduce in our way, viable recombinations of damage would be rare. A "baby car" that inherited a flat tire from its "mother" and a damaged fuel pump from its "father" would be less efficient than either of its "parents." In man, mutations produce dwarfism, albinism, hemophilia, polydactyly, various forms of idiocy, about half of all cases of blindness and deafness, certain features of diabetes, epilepsy, heart disease, cerebral palsy, arthritis, and so on. A sudden increase in the rate of mutation would increase the frequency of these afflictions and *decrease* the proportion of healthy individuals in the population as a whole, reducing the fecundity of mankind. It would not, in itself, alter or affect the actual *course* of human evolution. This would be determined by natural selection, through the random "selection" of viable gene combinations from the mass of genes available. Professor Crow estimated that the ideal rate of mutation for the foreseeable future in *Homo sapiens* would be zero.

Most evolutionary change is brought about by *recombination* of the genes already available in the population.

This is the biological function of sex. If all mutation should cease today, a vast range of evolutionary changes would still be open to man. The number of different gene combinations that could be produced by the present world population exceeds the estimated number of electrons in the visible universe. In any one set of environmental conditions (for example, those of today), many of these possible combinations of genes (that is, people) would be unable to survive. Under different conditions, however, combinations that are now harmful would become beneficial. If man could survive only in the stygian darkness of deep caves, eyes would be rendered useless and senses like touch and hearing would become more important. Cave-dwelling animals of many kinds have become pale in color and their eyes have either disappeared or persist only as nonfunctional vestiges.

Another feature of mutation that is often overlooked is the fact that it is *recurrent*. The same mutations occur again and again, in New Zealand, Japan, New York, and Timbuctu. Some of the very same ones were taking place in ancient Greeks, and even in Peking man. The supply of mutations is maintained constantly. Even those that kill are not lost as a possible source of evolutionary change, for they will recur again and again. In some unforeseen future environment they might cease to kill, and become valuable components of the interacting genes of the individuals able to survive in that environment. The harmful or beneficial features of genes are not inherent in the genes themselves, nor unrelated to the environment around them. A gene that works well under one set of conditions may be a dead loss under another, rather as an absentminded professor might be useful in a large modern nation but a damn nuisance in a band of australopithecines.* "Beneficial" mutations are not permanently beneficial in some mysterious, metaphysical way, even though many modern biologists seem to think they are.

Overemphasis on mutation as an evolutionary force more or less in and of itself is apparent in Robert Ardrey's predictions of the results of a nuclear war. He says that if mankind was not wiped out altogether, the increased rate of mutation would be likely to produce a "new species." Actually, the likelihood of a new species would be *decreased* by a drastic increase in the rate of mutation. Natural selection would have *fewer* viable genes and gene combinations from which to "select" a new species. The fecundity of mankind would be drastically reduced at the very time when it would be most needed for survival. Extinction would be more likely than the appearance of a new species.

Ardrey rules out *Paranthropus* as a possible ancestor of man on the grounds that "mutations by the dozen" would have been required for the transformation. He is thinking of mutation in the sense of a saltation, or a sudden "big mutation." He says the human teeth and

---

* Our absentminded scientists now concoct such gruesome social problems as nuclear weapons, biological warfare, air and water and soil pollution, and overpopulation. They leave these social problems for others to solve and return to their crucibles to concoct even more. As Carleton Coon (1963, p. 126) points out, "scientists who know nothing but science can imperil the safety of the world."

smooth cranium of *Australopithecus africanus* "left him with only a single mutation — enlargement of the brain and consequent flattening of the face — to project him across the human threshold." Actually, such an incredibly enormous mutation is almost infinitely unlikely. In the genetic sense, a mutation is a *sudden*, more or less random, change in genetic material. Most geneticists discarded the old saltation theory fifty years ago, but even if we accept it for the sake of the present argument, it means that, if *Homo sapiens* crossed the human threshold in such a single enormous mutation, an australopithecine mother gave birth to a modern human baby. Even under the old saltation theory a mutation was a *sudden* change, and a gradual increase in the amazing physical complexity of the brain — from the australopithecine to the human level — is not a mutation. It is a very large-scale evolutionary change, involving billions of mutations and, above all, *natural selection* acting with tremendous force throughout the entire process. The supply of variability was maintained continuously by *recombination*, as each new generation of babies was born. Many of the most "superior" babies would have carried no "new" mutations at all. They would have received new *combinations* of genes which interacted in a way that produced more efficient brains.

GENETIC DRIFT

One of the world's leading authorities on evolution, Sewall Wright, considers mutation, migration, selection, inbreeding, and other factors, as a single complex system of forces.* All these forces interact simultaneously to produce what we call evolution. He has introduced a concept called "drift" into evolutionary thought. In very general terms, he means by this that small component groups of a large population tend to "drift apart" genetically, whether the climate or food supply changes or not. He does not suggest that the climate, food supply, et cetera, remain constant, or that they do not force animals to change genetically — he sees natural selection acting forcefully all the time. But he does contend that even in a stable and uniform external environment, small component groups of a large population would tend to become genetically different. This is very important, because natural selection will act far more quickly if it can select from a supply of rather large genetic differences that is being re-created constantly and rapidly.

Mutation alone will ensure that selection will always have a supply of genetic differences to choose from. But evolution would be a very slow and risky process if

* See *Encyclopaedia Britannica,* 1950 and 1968 editions, under "Genetics of Populations."

mutation was the *only* source of genetic variation.* Certain other processes vastly increase the rate at which genetic differences are re-created. Sex is one of these. Through sex a new array of genetic diversity is produced with every generation. New "hands of genes," as it were, are dealt out all around. Superimposed on mutation, sex increases the rate of production of genetic diversity enormously. Sewall Wright has described processes which, superimposed on *both* mutation *and* sex, increase the rate of production of genetic diversity *even more*.

Wright means something more by "drift" than the restricted aspect of the concept usually described in modern high school texts under the heading of "drift," or "the Sewall Wright Effect." He means any and all of the factors that tend to increase genetic differences between small groups of a large population — including selection due to slight local differences in climate, food supply, et cetera.

A hypothetical example of Wright's concept of drift is a large population of australopithecines, broken up into many little social groups, all fairly well segregated from one another. Wright has not used such an example himself, and has not applied his concept of drift directly to humans or subhumans, but this example will serve our purposes very well. There will be some exchange of individuals between our little groups of australopithecines, but like baboons they will be tending to hold themselves together in small well-knit bands of friends and relations.

* That is, if all living things reproduced themselves asexually, as do the body cells of a growing organism.

Now and then a traded or stolen female will pass from one group to another, but most of the individuals will keep to their own kind. Under these conditions, friends will tend to become relatives in a very real and close genetic sense. If each little group contains only about a hundred individuals, and holds itself more or less together as an integrated unit for several generations, first cousins will mate with first cousins, unless they are able to capture or lure mates from another group. Baboon groups keep a close watch on their own females, especially when two groups are near one another at a water hole. Human groups also keep an eye on their females, and sometimes react as violently as Simeon and Levi did when some foreigner trifles with one of them. Under such conditions and under the duress of powerful urges, even brothers and sisters, or fathers and daughters, may mate with each other. Dogs and baboons seem to have no scruples about incest, and the brother-sister marriages of ancient Egypt are well known. Even Cleopatra was engaged, in accordance with Egyptian custom, to marry her younger brother — before Julius Caesar arrived with all the charms of the Roman Empire. Brother-sister marriages were also common in the ruling families of Polynesia. Even the ruling families of Europe have dabbled in inbreeding from time to time, though they drew the line outside the brother-sister relationship.

As everyone knows, extreme inbreeding tends to produce imbeciles and other kinds of unfortunate children. Most people — apart from plant and animal breeders — are less well aware of the fact that inbreeding also produces very "superior" animals. All our "pure breeds" of pets, livestock, vegetables, et cetera, are inbred to some considerable extent — and in order to keep the qualities of each breed from melting away before our eyes, we have to continue this inbreeding. Pedigreed bitches are closely guarded by owners who wish to sell pedigreed pups. The mating of a pedigreed poodle with another pedigreed poodle is a form of inbreeding, even when the two poodles are not even first cousins. There is no sharp line between inbreeding and outbreeding so far as evolution is concerned, but most animal breeders draw arbitrary lines and reserve the term for a more or less close inbreeding. The genetic reasons for both the imbeciles and the "superior" individuals that result from inbreeding are well understood, but we need not go into them here in detail. In very general terms, inbreeding brings together in the same individuals both the "good" and the "bad" genes of their parents. Harmful genes that were "masked" by other genes in the parents may appear in "double dose" in their inbred offspring, sometimes with disastrous effects. These very casualties, however, tend to "purge" the breed of its harmful genes as inbreeding continues over the generations. The good genes also tend to appear in double dose in inbred offspring, and once a breed has been purged of its bad genes and has gathered together most of its good genes in double doses, the breed has been more or less "purified," and we call it a "pure" breed. Humans who fancy themselves genetically sometimes refer to themselves as "blue bloods," and sometimes even imply that their ancestors have been closely inbred all the way back to William the Conqueror.

Each little social group of our large population of australopithecines, then, will be inbreeding rather closely. But each of them will be "purifying" itself in a different genetic direction. In one of them, for example, most individuals may have rather large noses simply because they are all descended from a greedy grandfather who had a big nose and an even bigger harem (which included his own daughters as well as the two "foreign" females he had managed to steal, at great risk, from an enemy group). This enemy group, on the other hand, may have rather small noses, on the average, simply because *their* greedy grandfather had a small nose. The difference in nose size between these two groups may have little or nothing to do with the climate, or food supply, or natural selection in the knock-'em-down-and-drag-'em-out sense. Even the genes in the two grandfathers that helped them to maintain their little harems, despite the desires of their deprived sons, may have produced the two noses only incidentally, as unimportant side effects. But each grandfather would have had other qualities also, quite apart from his nose, and the genes that helped him to develop these qualities would also have been passed on to his descendants. Nearly all these descendants would have some of these genes, and they would therefore tend to be more or less alike, mentally and emotionally, as well as physically. Each little group would, in fact, be moving blindly in the direction of a pure breed. It will never get there, however, because something will surely happen to disturb the even tenor of its isolationist ways before too many generations have passed.

Each group, then, will be moving toward a "pure breed" condition, but each will be moving in a different genetic direction, and each will have a different "pedigree," or genetic background. We therefore have uniformity within each group and diversity between different groups taking place at one and the same time. This sort of thing can confuse us if we concentrate too closely on one aspect of the process and overlook the other. Inbreeding tends toward uniformity, but it also tends toward diversity *at the same time*. We must remember that each little australopithecine group will be more or less genetically uniform inside itself, but also that all the little social groups will be more different genetically than they would have been if they had all been exchanging females with gay abandon. Therefore, we have a genetic between-group diversity that will appear even if the climate, food supply, et cetera, remain very much the same. The inbreeding will be augmented by other factors, such as the loss of certain genes by random accidents, or acts of God, which have nothing to do with the evolutionary "value" of those genes. Sperms carrying replicates of a particular gene may have a run of pure luck at finding and fertilizing eggs, and hence these genes may be more numerous in future generations purely because of this run of luck. Other genes may disappear from a particular group because of a run of *bad* luck. Many modern biologists restrict Wright's concept of drift within the rather narrow limits of these runs of good and bad luck. Wright himself, however, means more than this, as pointed out above.

Nearly all modern biologists have accepted Wright's basic theory. Disputes are largely quibbles over its details. Given the subdivision of a population into many small subgroups, ideally with about a hundred or fewer individuals in each; given a limited amount of migration, or exchange of individuals between groups; given the inbreeding that must take place under such conditions; add a pinch of genetic roulette in terms of random runs of luck for certain genes — and the result will be a far greater array of genetic diversity than would be present in a highly mobile population where every individual came and went and mated willy-nilly.

HUMAN DIVERSITY

Group segregation is still at a very high level in New Guinea. The total number of mutually unintelligible languages may be about eight hundred, in an area comparable to that of France and Great Britain combined. The average New Guinea native is able to converse fluently with less than four thousand people. In order to grasp what this means in terms of social isolation, imagine yourself in a small village of several hundred illiterate people, surrounded on all sides by similar villages — either hostile or precariously allied with your own. In an area of about 375 square miles (for example, a square twenty miles long on each side) the villagers speak a language allied to your own, but in the more remote villages, even within this small area, they speak with a dialect that you can barely understand. Beyond this area, all people speak languages you find quite unintelligible. Your social contacts with the world at large would then be roughly equal to those of the average New Guinea native today.

Matthiessen describes the outlook of a people who live in the Baliem River valley, in the Snow Mountains region of western New Guinea: "The Baliem lay in the countries of the enemy, and though it was less than four miles distant, at the far end of the Siobara, the children would never know more of it than the fringe of casuarina which hid its waters from their sight."

According to Reed there is so little integration among native social aggregates larger than villages in New Guinea that the participants in a "common culture" can hardly be considered as a "tribe." The Manus of the Admiralty Islands, for example, share a homogeneous culture and a common language. They number about two thousand people in all, in eleven settlements (an average of about 182 per settlement), but there are few social connections and no common political organization among the separate settlements. "Only in war," Reed says, "or on the rare occasions of intervillage feasts do villages participate as units."

There is a considerable volume of evidence suggesting that a prehistoric pattern of humans living in many small well-segregated social groups has persisted into very recent times. Australian aborigines, American Indians, Kalahari Bushmen, Congo Pygmies, and many others, were segregated into small social groups. Exchanges took place between these, but they were not frequent enough to break down the social, *and genetic*, distinctions between them. Carleton Coon says the American Indians were more homogeneous physically than any other continental population; even the Australian aborigines were more divergent. This tallies with available evidence on the timing of the first invasions of America. A mere ten thousand years or so was simply not enough time for the evolution, from a small nucleus of original immigrants, of genetic differences comparable to those on other continents. But an impressive array of differences developed nevertheless. Mason describes a remarkable thoracic development and chest expansion in the inhabitants of the high Peruvian plateau. The blood volume of these people is nearly two quarts greater than that of "normal" humans, they have almost twice as much hemoglobin as sea-level dwellers, and their red blood count is about eight millions as compared with about five millions for Europeans living at low altitudes. Their pulse rate is also remarkably slow. This striking evolutionary change took place in less than ten thousand years.

Many additional examples could be cited, but these should be sufficient to convey the general idea. Group size and intergroup contacts were probably greater in recent than in early humans, and if so, genetic diversity between early human groups was even greater than that which remains apparent today. There is no scarcity of genetic diversity upon which natural selection can act to-day, and there was almost certainly a comparable diver-sity in early humans. Learning capacities can hardly be identical in all groups when so many physical and other features are, and certainly were, so obviously diverse. Hu-man brain efficiency has increased during the past two million years, and it is ridiculous to assume that at every single stage of the entire process the mental efficiency of all human groups was always so precisely equal that natu-ral selection had no variation upon which to act. Yet this is precisely what some highly qualified scientists claim.

HUMAN EQUALITY

The UNESCO statement on race, as cited by Lasker, reads as follows: "Available scientific knowledge provides no basis for believing that the groups of mankind differ in their innate capacity for intellectual and emotional de-velopment."

This statement illustrates not only a capacity for glo-bal cooperation but also a desire for it. Perhaps this de-sire may account for the fact that the statement is easily misunderstood. Let us study it closely. The "groups of mankind" is a loose term that could mean anything from small subgroups within a town to groups of nations or races. Since the statement is "on race," we can probably assume that it refers to large racial groups. Teachers and parents and the authors of the UNESCO statement all know that *individuals* differ in their "innate" capacities for intellectual and emotional development. Some children are born with defective genetic material, as in the case of several kinds of idiocy. All individuals differ genetically (apart from identical twins) and therefore all *groups* of individuals differ genetically. Brains and endocrine systems determine, and limit, capacities for intellectual and emotional development. Brains and endocrine systems are produced by the action of genes, and hence the capacities in question are also determined, and limited, by genes.

Modern scientists define the word *innate* in genetic terms. Since all individuals and groups differ genetically, their capacities for intellectual and emotional development also differ genetically, or innately. Lyndon Johnson and Barry Goldwater differ in their innate capacities for intellectual and emotional development, and all the Democrats differ innately from all the Republicans, both individually and as two separate groups. When considering examples of this kind our feelings are likely to become emotional rather than scientific. But scientific knowledge *does* provide a basis for believing that the differences exist. Science does *not* provide a basis for beliefs as to which is "best," except in extreme cases where we have clearly stated the *particular* attributes to which we are referring. A group of children who received defective genes that impair the efficiency of their brains will differ from other groups of children in their innate capacities to learn higher mathematics. When comparing the population of China with that of Great Britain, however, we can say only that they *differ*, genetically, and thus also in their innate capacities for intellectual and emotional development — we cannot say which is "superior" or "inferior" to the other.

The UNESCO statement is framed in very broad and general terms; it includes *all* kinds of intellectual and emotional development simultaneously. This vastly increases the likelihood that all human groups *differ*. Two football teams from neighboring towns may have exactly the same *average* skull capacity. This is very unlikely, but it is not inconceivable. It is less likely that they will average exactly the same in skull capacity *and* in their ability to compose music. It is almost infinitely unlikely that they will average exactly the same in these *two* characteristics *and* in their ability to build bridges, settle disputes, kill enemies, court females, and so on ad infinitum.

No sharp lines can be drawn between human races. At least some interbreeding has taken place between most of them. In the case of Caucasians, Negroes, and Chinese, however, we can point to readily visible physical differences that are known to be genetically determined. Chinese parents do not produce Negro babies, or vice versa. The physical differences between these three large racial groups are many and diverse. They appear, however, in recognizable *patterns*: despite the extreme variability within each group, its own complex *pattern* of characteristics is stamped clearly on nearly all its individuals. Young children easily learn to recognize these patterns. The physical differences between these three races reflect complex differences in their relative abilities to cope with certain features of the physical environment. We cannot measure or assess these differences, even though we know they must exist. They are multidimensional, and we are dealing with averages and large samples rather than individuals. It is entirely reasonable to assume that patterns of genetic differences affect the brains and endocrine systems of Negroes, Caucasians, and Chinese, as well as the external features that we can see. Here again, we cannot measure these differences, but we know they exist. Sir Julian Huxley (1963, p. 297) implies that intelligence may have a strong genetic component, and claims that the increased social and cultural efficiency resulting from even a small difference in the number of outstandingly gifted people is very important in considering the problem of possible racial differences. He conveys the impression that he has not accepted the UNESCO statement in a final or absolute sense.

A "racist" is one who believes his own race is superior (or inferior*) to other races. As we all know, there are white, yellow, and black racists pronouncing such doctrines. The brutal history of the slave trade, and the superman doctrines of Nietzsche and Hitler, have produced a strong reaction and an opposing group of "antiracists" who preach a doctrine of equality that feeds on such "proof" as the UNESCO statement. The desire for a world brotherhood of all racial groups is laudable, and the realization of this desire is essential to our survival as

* A form of "inverted racism" is common among people who have been overwhelmed by a more complex civilization or technology, and it appears in such guises as hair straightening, surgical removal of eye folds, and emphasis on skin color in marriage arrangements.

a species. But we are less likely to achieve such a brotherhood if we align ourselves into two hostile groups, each defending its own half-truth with fervent devotion. Let us not forget that we belong to the only animal species that has built a hydrogen bomb.

SHEEP, GOATS, AND NATURAL SELECTION

We cannot say which race is "best"; we have difficulty enough grading the examination results of students. But natural selection, acting for two million years, has been far more efficient than we will ever be at separating sheep from goats. The vast majority of all the species that have lived on this earth have left no living descendants. Given the vast genetic diversity that emerges naturally between countless thousands of little social groups, due to inbreeding, et cetera, natural selection has something to get its teeth into, both literally and figuratively. Some little groups will have far "better" genes than others and these genetic inequalities will make themselves felt in terms of unequal rates of reproduction. Sewall Wright's model is a thoroughly peaceful one (he was not referring to *Homo sapiens* in particular). Even without war, it is generally agreed that the genes of the more successful groups will be favored by natural selection, and will therefore tend to spread throughout the species by means of migration. *Homo sapiens* is the only animal species that fights intergroup wars with malice aforethought. (Social insects may be excluded on the arrogant grounds that they are incapable of forethoughts.)

In our australopithecine population, some little groups will be tending toward imbecility, and their days will be numbered. Other groups will be moving in a "blue-blood" direction. Inequalities in the distribution of food and water and females will promote social unrest, and our entire array of little social groups will start moving around, looking for greener pastures and female variety. Whenever a blue-blooded group finds an imbecilic group enjoying the fruits of a tiny garden of Eden, we can be confident that it will move in and take over. If the imbeciles resist, they will be opposed by some primeval ancestor of Alexander's phalanx formation. They might reduce the genetic potential of the blue-blooded group slightly by killing a few of its warriors, but if they lose *all* their own males, the genetic potential of the two groups combined will increase. The victorious warriors will acquire even bigger harems, if any of the imbecilic females catch their eye in the heat of battle. They will continue to mate with their *own* females, thereby rapidly recovering the genetic loss of their fallen comrades, and they will also infuse genetic crumbs into the conquered concubines.

This is natural selection in its most raw and brutal form. Australopithecines were not "created equal," any more than we are today — and their natures were probably no more gentle when they found other australopithecines standing between them and the desires of their

K

hearts than we are now when we see horns sprouting from the heads of our enemies. The fact that we are beginning to get a little squeamish as we sit under our nuclear umbrellas may be one of the more hopeful results of human evolution — provided it does not blind us from reality altogether. Ethically, it is very good of us to tell each other that all tribes are equal, but this will not alter the fact that we are all different.

The facts of life are savage and primeval, and we are the most savage animals on earth. If we can face — like men — the fact that we are animals, we might be able to see more clearly how it is that we are also the most intelligent and sympathetic of all animals. But we will never see ourselves clearly unless we can learn to look at both sides of ourselves at once. If we cling to one side so passionately that we blind ourselves to the other, we stand in danger of calling each other names — and this arouses emotions that we have inherited from australopithecines.

VI

CAVALRY AND BATTLESHIPS

MAN HAS ALWAYS BEEN A MOBILE ANIMAL;
he made the long journey from Bering Strait to Cape
Horn on foot, with only occasional help from floating
logs and primitive canoes. But the advent of ships and
horses greatly increased man's mobility, and this must
have had a powerful effect on his evolution. Any increase
in mobility would quicken the tempo in the "hot center"
model already described. Exposure to sudden attacks
from faraway places would pose very serious problems. A
Norwegian fjord, or an island in the Aegean or Pacific,
may have been a haven of peace — until longships and
war canoes began to arrive silently out of the dawn. At
this point, the dwellers in such former hideouts were
suddenly living on a highway. They were caught on the
horns of a dilemma. Should they increase their faith in
the gentleness of the inner natures of primitive men —
and risk being killed or enslaved if their faith was unfounded? Or should they head for the hills and hide in
the thickets? Or should they build ships of their own and

prepare to repel boarders — that is, get organized and *mobilized?*

Greater mobility increases the rate of extermination or banishment of less cooperative groups, and facilitates the realization of any capacities for really large-scale cooperation that may have been evolved. The Roman Empire was held together by the roads that led to Rome, and Menes of Egypt could not have imposed social cohesion along the Nile without ships. Mobility elongates the arms of law and order, but it also imposes powerful demands on the *efficiency* of law and order. Large bodies of men are not easily controlled, even when they have no means of conveyance other than legs and feet, as the Army of the Potomac learned more than once from Stonewall Jackson's "foot cavalry" during the American Civil War. When every man is mounted on a horse, central control can be even more difficult. Cooperation within an "empire" must always be maintained by a difficult balance between *forceful* coercion and *voluntary* obedience. Savage men do not submit to gentle pleas from weak philosophers, and armies of slaves under the lash do not fight with the berserk ferocity of Huns or Vikings.

If increased mobility did in fact increase the rate of removal of the least cooperative groups, large-scale social cooperation should have appeared first in association with boats and horses. History suggests that boats led the way. The earliest civilizations appeared along the Nile, the Tigris-Euphrates, the Indus, and the Hwang Ho rivers. We cannot "prove" that riverboats increased the rate of removal of ineffectual brains, but the fact remains that civilizations first appeared along these rivers. If greater mobility quickens the rate of human evolution, then the horsemen of central Asia should not have lagged behind the rest of mankind — and the evidence of history suggests they did not. Wave after wave of horsemen rolled in from the steppelands of Asia — to found a succession of civilizations in China, India, the Near East, and Europe. More than one ruling élite was descended from nomadic great-grandfathers. The vast grasslands could be exploited more effectively by shifting herds of livestock over great distances, and therefore cities did not appear on the steppes. But the men who survived on this open terrain obeyed their leaders with a voluntary enthusiasm that made the blood of untold millions of townsmen run cold.

HORSES

Just before the dawn of history, true horses seem to have been unknown in the Near East. Asses and onagers (a larger species of wild ass) were native to the Near East, but they had less military potential than the horse, and horses were native to central Asia. Heavy war carts with solid wheels, drawn by horselike animals (probably onagers), were depicted in early Sumer around 3000 B.C., but the true horse was "broken in" in central Asia.

According to E. D. Phillips most of central Asia west

of Zungaria was inhabited by white men in ancient times. He says that mongoloids hardly appear on this western half of the steppes before the "Hunnish" movement during the last centuries B.C. Zungaria was near the Altai Mountains, south of the headwaters of the Yenesei River. The Yenesei runs due north through Siberia to enter the Arctic Ocean east of Novaya Zemlya. Europeans may wish to consult a map and admire the immensity of the area their ancestors had conquered so long ago. The Altai Mountains lie three thousand miles east of the Danube, and only about twelve hundred miles northwest of the Hwang Ho. White nomads were seen on the northwest border of China during the first millennium B.C., and the terrible Huns and Mongols of later centuries carried a mixture of "white" and "yellow" genes. The advent of the horse greatly accelerated the rate of gene exchange between the two major races of northern Eurasia. The initial divergence had evolved in the isolation of the foot-slogging days. The first riders of the steppes seem to have been caucasoid (possibly with enough mongoloid genes to provide a trace of "hybrid vigor").

True horses appeared in Babylonia around 2000 B.C., when the Tripolye culture was disappearing from southern Russia. Indo-Europeans were appearing in the Near East — like bubbles in a pot of water that will soon begin to boil. Stuart Piggott says the scribes of Akkad, around 2000 B.C., described the appearance of "the Amorite who knows not grain, a host whose onslaught was like a hurricane, a people who had never known a city." In the chaotic confusion of a hurricane it is not easy to keep track of people, and the swirling admixture of genes can quickly obscure racial origins. F. M. T. Böhl * says the Israelites believed the Amorites to be a race of giants, and that Egyptian illustrations showed them as long-headed and blue-eyed, with straight noses and thin lips. When they arrived in Palestine they were clearly connected in some way with Indo-Europeans,† in the ethnic sense, but they were absorbed rapidly and intimately into the Semitic populations of the region. Böhl says the Hyksos invasion of Egypt was probably related to the appearance of these nomads in Syria and Palestine, and that their Amoritic language was an earlier stage of the Hebrew language.

William Albright says that during the eighteenth and seventeenth centuries B.C. (1800–1600) the people east of the Jordan River became almost entirely nomadic, and that the first Semitic precursors of the Hyksos irruption probably came from Palestine well before 1700 B.C. He says a great southward migration of Indo-Aryans and Horites (Hurrians) seems "increasingly probable" soon after 1700 B.C. There is no trace of these racial elements in Palestine and northern Syria before 1700, but Indo-Aryan and Horite princes and nobles were established "almost everywhere" (in Palestine) during the next two

* *Encyclopaedia Britannica,* 1950 edition, Vol. 1, pp. 829–830.

† *Indo-European* is a linguistic term, applied to the ancestral languages that gave rise to the dominant languages of today's Europe, northern India, Russia, North and South America, Australia, New Zealand, and much of Africa. The term should not really be used in an ethnic sense, but the relationship between European languages and Europeans remains overwhelmingly obvious.

centuries. The fact that the invaders became princes and nobles is highly pertinent to the present argument, and they seem to have swamped the Near East even more quickly than their descendants flooded over North America. Albright says, "we must picture the northern hordes as sweeping through Palestine and Egypt in swift chariots, with footmen playing a strictly subordinate role." When horses thundered into the Near East the very earth began to heave upward — rather like a thick porridge beginning to boil. Albright says "great fortifications of beaten earth" arose all over Syria and Palestine.

The Hyksos invasion brought the horse and the chariot to Egypt, along with an infusion of combined Semitic and Amoritic genes. Soon afterward, Joseph rose to prominence there and the Israelites multiplied in the land of Goshen. Were it not for the testimony of the Bible, one could suspect that they entered Egypt in the wake of invading Hyksos horsemen, rather than peacefully under the auspices of the ruling Pharaoh. If their language was really Amoritic, they may have been an actual component of the Hyksos invasion. But the Biblical account rules out this possibility.

During this same general period, horsemen called Aryans rode into India and laid the foundations of India's present upper caste. The Shang dynasty was founded in China with the aid of chariots and horses. Redoubtable Hittite chariots appeared in Anatolia. Horses entered Greece and appeared on the island of Crete and penetrated Africa. Mobile men of the steppes were on the move from China to Europe. These were the days of the chariot, not of mounted cavalry — but even so, the effect of horses and horsemen was cataclysmic. Even with their windpipes pinched by a poorly designed harness, these faithful early horses moved the bronze swords and the battle-axes fast enough to clear the field of many uncooperative people.

Horses quickened the tempo of history throughout the second millennium B.C., but near its close they produced the enormous explosion described in chapter IV. Shortly before the motley tribes of Greece and the Aegean were transformed into desperate "Peoples of the Sea," men on the steppes of central Asia had learned to place one foot in a stirrup and swing the other up over the back of a horse. Freed from the restricting influence of pinched windpipes, the horses carried the bows and the swords and battle-axes (now made of iron) with the speed of an avalanche, and spread the genes of their riders over most of Eurasia. The explosion of the late second millennium was only the first of a long series of irruptions of *mounted* men into Europe and India and China, and a succession of kingdoms and empires and ruling aristocracies followed each wave of invading horsemen.

In the west, the horses carried caucasoid genes for nearly a thousand years — in Iranians, Scythians, Sakas, Sarmatians, Parthians, and others. The genes of the Aryan Iranians were recombined to form the Medes and Persians who built roads and suppressed petty warfare for three thousand miles, from Egypt to India. The ten thousand Immortals of the Persian army were all cavalry-men. Cyrus and Darius and Xerxes were descended directly from nomadic horsemen — and they were not as evil as the histories of their little Greek enemies have led us to believe. We do not know how far these nomadic caucasoid genes penetrated into Europe, or how quickly they became diluted there — but men were invading Italy when the Aryans rode into Iran and India, and white nomads were appearing on the northwestern borders of China. The overall flow of genes was *outward*, from central Asia. The flow in the opposite direction was relatively slight. Neither Darius nor Alexander conquered the Scythians of southern Russia, and Roman Legions under Crassus were shot to bits by Saka bowmen of the Parthian army. Chinese expeditions penetrated the steppelands occasionally, but like those of Darius and Alexander and Crassus they always recoiled backward into less open terrain. When they returned to China they were followed more than once by hordes of cavalrymen, who then ruled over them for generations.

When horses began to carry human genes, people moved so far and so fast, and pressures from central Asia were so fiercely persistent and powerful, that a strong flow of genes must have been infused into the very heart of Europe. Phillips says there are Royal Scyth tombs on the Danubian plain, and that single outlier Scythian graves occur in northern Germany. Tamara Rice speaks of adventurous groups of Scythians "restlessly pushing ever farther towards the west" — through Hungary. These invaders would not have remained "pure," of course. They were polygamous men with an eye for female variety. All their descendants would have received half of their genes from their mothers. But the men who were still fighting with obsolete chariots in Britannia when Caesar arrived there may well have inherited more than this habit from the Russian steppes. Blond Vikings whose skins were nailed to the doors of churches in Saxon England may have inherited more than the color of their hair from blond nomadic ancestors who rode north from Hungary.

During the final centuries of the pre-Christian era, mongoloid genes began to mingle with caucasoid genes on the backs of horses on the northern and western borders of China. A vast array of new gene combinations appeared on the face of the earth, scattered in enormous variety over the steppes, from Tibet to Manchuria. Presented with this sudden explosion of genetic variety, natural selection became even more swift and savage. Horses thundered in all directions and swarms of arrows flicked from bows, thumping into those gene combinations that failed to meet the merciless demands of social cooperation. Unsuccessful gene combinations were eliminated with terrible speed, and those that survived were eventually called the Scourge of God by untold millions of Chinese and Europeans.

E. D. Phillips says that from Chinese records it appears that as late as the fifth century B.C. the nomads of the Gobi region were still unmounted and easily defeated by charioteers. But by 300 B.C., he says, they were expert cavalrymen. Tamara Rice says the male skulls and mummified heads from the Pazirik tombs of the High Altai were mostly caucasoid, but that one chieftain and one woman were mongoloid. In these tombs nomads related to Scythians buried their chieftains under stone-topped barrows, the contents of which have been frozen in ice — for more than twenty-three centuries. Normally perishable objects, including human bodies, were thus preserved in good condition since about 400 B.C. The skill and care that had been devoted to bridles and bits and other horse gear was clearly apparent in the contents of these graves, and the artistic talents of the nomads of this remote region were more remarkable than was previously suspected. The mongoloid chieftain had been buried with a tall woman of European type who had long, soft, wavy black hair. Her brain and entrails had been removed and replaced with plant materials, after which the skull had been replaced and the scalp and abdomen sewn up again. The mongoloid man had been killed in battle by two axe strokes, and scalped. His own men had apparently recovered his body and sewed on a false scalp to replace the one he had lost. The man had also been embalmed with plant material, and the process was exactly as described by Herodotus for the Scythians. This evidence could hardly show more clearly that mongoloid and caucasoid genes were being intermingled just before the Gobi nomads began to attack China in cavalry formations. The Pazirik tombs show also that, at least in that area, the genetic mixing had only just begun.

Phillips says the Hsiung Nu were first mentioned in Chinese annals around 200 B.C. The Great Wall had already been built by that time, so the annals seem to have been referring to attacks of an earlier date. The Hsiung

Nu had adopted a very powerful bow, stiffened with plates of bone. Their cavalry fought expertly, in an improved version of the Sarmatian style which had driven the Scythians from southern Russia. They reached their greatest power soon after 200 B.C., when a chief named Mao-tun defeated the Yueh Chi tribe to the west of his territory. This Yueh Chi tribe had once been stronger than the Hsiung Nu, and it seems to have been a composite horde, led by a "royal tribe of Iranians" who ruled over a genetic conglomeration of "Tocharians" and "Turks." The flight of the Yueh Chi toward the west, around 160 B.C., set off a chain reaction that would eventually shatter the Roman Empire and send a succession of waves of genes to far-off Britain, Spain, and North Africa.

The empire of the Hsiung Nu, who dominated the heart of this hot center, extended for two thousand miles, from Korea to the Altai Mountains. A census of all livestock in this vast area was carried out each year, at a time when the Romans had only heard vague reports of a foggy island in the northern seas that would later be known as Britannia — and when the inhabitants of that island were ill informed about the livestock beyond their own little clearings in the woods. The Hsiung Nu were no mere horde of disorganized barbarians — they had developed a very elaborate system of government. Their social coordination was effective enough to send shivers coursing up and down the spines of Han emperors in China for centuries. They branded upon the temperament of China a habit of concern with her northern frontier, and their brand was so hot that the habit persists to this day. Their name, in the garbled form of "Huns," echoed over six thousand miles, all the way to France — and over two thousand years, to the trenches of World War I. Other men have been savage and barbaric, but few have been socially organized on such a colossally potent scale.

The Hsiung Nu who threatened China were not the Huns that transformed the genetic makeup of Europe, but both "hordes" were a conglomeration of mongoloid and caucasoid gene combinations. The Chinese described the Hsiung Nu as hairy men with large noses, and the Europeans described the Huns as mongoloid. E. D. Phillips concludes from this that the Huns who invaded Europe were more mongoloid than the rest of the vast array of combinations between the two races. But this seems unlikely. As the genes of the Yueh Chi flowed westward over the centuries the mongoloid component would have been increasingly diluted in a more and more caucasoid "genetic soup." The reverse should have happened to the caucasoid genes in the Hsiung Nu as they flowed back and forth over northern China. Neither the Chinese nor the Europeans carried out a calm and careful study of the ethnic characteristics of the horsemen who were slaughtering them. The Hsiung Nu and the Huns were evil incarnate in the eyes of Chinese and Europeans alike. It is therefore not surprising that they both saw *foreign* features in their frightful foes. When men are under the influence of extreme terror and hatred, they do not look for the features of their friends in the faces of enemies as savage as the Hsiung Nu or the Huns.

The nomadic tribes of central Asia were not always united. More often they were divided into many small interhostile groups, and at such times the more settled civilizations of China and India and Europe enjoyed interludes of relative peace and security. While the terrible striking power of the nomadic cavalry was being dissipated in thousands of petty little interclan and intertribal wars, the settled civilizations could lapse into the illusion that the threat from the steppes had evaporated. The vast reaches of inner Asia could be forgotten. They had never been known, in any case, except as a mysterious source of savage hordes. The Great Unknown of the remote hinterlands could recede into the vague limbo of memory, to be revived only rarely in the flickering firelight, while some old man or woman told dreamlike tales of incredible warriors and unbelievable massacres. China and India and Europe could sleep again. But the threat from the steppes had not evaporated. Genghis Khan was born during one of these interludes.

When the nomads were not actually threatening settled peoples, they were applying the white heat of their furies to one another — and demanding, paradoxically, more efficient cooperation with one another. Their less capable warriors were being tempered in the fierce crucible of the open steppes: the two-pronged sweep of the well-planned raid, the false retreat, the sudden backward Parthian shot, and the swift coup de grace when the victims are lured well into the trap. Although neither the nomads nor their future victims knew it, this was an interlude of training, mobilization, and rapid natural selection.

Organized men have irrupted from the unknown entrails of Asia throughout historic times, and Cro-Magnon man seems to have entered Europe from the general direction of Asia some forty thousand years ago, when Neanderthal man became extinct. North America was first entered from the west — again from the general direction of central Asia — about ten thousand years ago. Most of these early movements are lost in the silence of the prehistoric tomb (and in the modern illusion that unbroken peace prevailed for millions of years). But the major source of migrating men became gradually discernible when the mysterious pulsations of peoples — from the east into Europe, and from the north and west into China and India — began to appear in the annals of history. After the fifth century explosion of the Huns, the source of these rivers of human genes was even more clearly revealed. Turkish Avars irrupted in the sixth century, Bulgars in the seventh and eighth, Magyars in the ninth, Pechenegs in the tenth, Kipchaks in the eleventh, and the Mongols of Genghis Khan in the thirteenth century.

Since his death in 1227 Genghis Khan has become a Hollywood movie star. He has bequeathed lucrative plots to modern writers, and his sons provided a powerful punch line for one of Winston Churchill's most famous speeches. Nearly all literate men have heard of Genghis Khan, but we all see him through a fog of emotion — and we do not yet understand the full implications of his remarkable career. During his lifetime he was a symbol of social cohesion for millions of nomads, and a Scourge of God for everyone else. When he was born, the nomads were too preoccupied with one another to be concerned with China or Poland, Russia or India, but during his lifetime they coalesced into one of the most enormous and complex systems of social cohesion that has ever appeared on the earth. The effects of this social organization were recorded in terror and horror by the pens of many literate men, and we see Genghis Khan and his Mongols as hordes of ruthless brutes, pursuing rapine and massacre with single-minded devotion and chilling efficiency. We see him through the eyes of his terrified enemies, and whenever we look outward from our love of "us" at the savagery of "them," we see a distortion of reality.

Genghis Khan and his Mongols were savage and cruel, as men have often been savage and cruel. Canaan was conquered and Carthage annihilated before he was born, the Inquisition began in earnest a few years after his death, and hydrogen bombs are being built today. But Mongols cannot be used effectively in large cavalry formations without social cooperation, any more than hydrogen bombs can be built single-handedly by one man. Social cooperation was the key to Genghis Khan's power, and this is the most distinctively human characteristic of man. Social cooperation cannot be achieved on a continental scale in the absence of many thousands of very complex and capable brains. Hordes of fierce and illiterate nomads are not easily organized, even with the aid of written orders and the stability of stationary cities, headquarters, courtrooms, and prisons. The efficiency of brains that can, without such help, coalesce into a single social system, sprawled over five thousand miles from Poland to China, must give us pause. We will not understand either ourselves or Genghis Khan if we see this phenomenon purely in terms of brute ferocity, as an uncontrollable manifestation of mindless endocrine instinct, or as an infiltration of devils into mongoloid "Gadarene swine."

Genghis Khan's armies were highly organized and superbly led. His campaigns were no random eruptions of barbaric rabble — they were carefully planned and very efficiently executed. His victories were not achieved by mere weight of numbers — his men were usually outnumbered by their opponents. B. H. Liddell Hart says the Mongols were more than a match for the warriors of medieval Europe, despite the numerical superiority and the heavier armor of the Europeans.* Contemporary observers of battles in Hungary were impressed with the speed, silence, and mechanical perfection of the Mongolian cavalry maneuvers, and with the deadly accuracy of their arrows. The Mongols never closed with an enemy until he was thoroughly weakened. When the heavy European cavalry charged, the Mongols dispersed on a silent flag signal, then rallied at another signal and resumed the deadly hail of arrows into their panting enemies. This was repeated with every European charge, until the Mongol commander judged his bleeding vic-

* *Encyclopaedia Britannica*, 1950 edition, Vol. 15, pp. 705–707.

tims ready for the kill, when the coup de grace was ordered silently and executed with a single devastating charge.

The Mongols did not fight in barbaric disorder on the battlefield, and they maintained a very strict law and order within their own ranks. It is said that anyone traveling under Mongolian auspices was able to move through Genghis Khan's vast empire from end to end without fear of molestation. The atrocities of the Mongols were as enormous as those of our own century, but they accomplished more than massacre and rapine. They demanded obedience with ruthless savagery, but they also established law and order over much of Eurasia.

The brains of Genghis Khan and his terrible men were able not only to learn large-scale social cooperation, but also to impose the habit on others. The empires they established followed the age-old pattern of disintegration — but like the ancient Persians, Romans, and Ch'in emperors of China, they left behind a concept of social unity that has never been forgotten. They left also an inheritance of *brains* that can be taught to think in terms of *global* unity (if they can be diverted from overpreoccupation with hydrogen bombs). Two of the most highly organized nations of history arose from the ruins of Genghis Khan's empire, and our hydrogen bombs are now aimed at and from central Asia.

Since the flow was mainly outward from central Asia, most of us now carry genes inherited from nomadic ancestors. A study of nomadic behavior might therefore help to relieve some of the baffled frustration that our social interactions produce today. It might also help us to understand why there were so many floods of people *away* from the steppes. Unfortunately, our nomadic ancestors were nearly always illiterate, and the few accounts we have of their social life were written by men who lacked firsthand knowledge of it. The behavior of foreigners is easily misunderstood, and it is often wise to discount the descriptions of our own social behavior that foreigners write while we are threatening them. It is always advisable to be cautious when we are considering people's descriptions of one another, and we must be *particularly* careful when we describe ourselves. However, we can probably accept the broad features of available accounts of nomadic behavior with reasonable confidence.

Our knowledge of the Indo-European Scythians who lived in southern Russia from about 700 to 200 B.C. is derived mainly from Herodotus, who wrote during the heyday of Scythian power. His descriptions have been discounted by certain scholars, but recent archaeological discoveries have revealed that many of his statements were surprisingly accurate. Herodotus says the Massagetae pursued the Cimmerians energetically enough to drive them out of both southern Russia and history. This tallies with information from other sources, and with the fact that men have been pursuing each other for thousands of years. Long after Herodotus died, the Scythians were themselves driven out of southern Russia by the

Sarmatians. Long after that, their descendants pursued the Indians across North America.

In very broad terms, then, Scythian social life was geared for dealing with foreign enemies; they fled from some, and expelled others from their ancestral homes. There is nothing unusual about this, but we often tend to forget it when we study human social behavior. The source of aggression is often sought in the individuals who lie on psychiatrists' couches, while the well-adjusted builders of hydrogen bombs are ignored. It is important to remember that fear of foreign aggression can influence the social behavior of *any* human group, and that this fear has been branded so deeply into our consciousness that we often fail to see it. Perhaps we are really so thoroughly permeated with fears of foreign aggression that we prefer to ignore them in the hope that they will go away (but we go on building our bombs, just in case). It is particularly important to remember this if we are to understand certain Scythian customs which might be described as shocking today.

Herodotus says the Scythians blinded their slaves, which seems unnecessarily barbaric. Having outlawed the more honest and less sophisticated forms of slavery, we tend to judge the superimposition of blinding on the crime of outright slavery as unforgivable. Such moral stone-casting is facilitated by the belief that human behavior emerges like an unsummoned genie from some mysterious source inside the *individual* — a source more or less unrelated to other individuals. If each individual

Scythian was *entirely* responsible for his own acts, if all
other people were entirely innocent, sharing no part of
the blame, then the Scythians were sadistic in their very
roots. Who wants to be descended from such unforgive-
ably evil ancestors? It is far more comforting to claim descent from imaginary pacifists who live in our dreams of
prehistoric peace. We recoil from the Scythians in horror, and under its influence we may feel such a powerful
urge to disbelieve Herodotus that we can drive the Roman arenas and the Nazi gas chambers out of our minds.
But if we can control ourselves, we might remember that
other unlikely seeming statements of Herodotus were
correct — and that this one is no more unlikely than
drawing and quartering, or boiling in oil.

Let us forget the fear of foreign aggression for a moment, and join Herodotus in seeking a smaller-scale explanation of slave-blinding. He says the practice was in
some way connected with the milking of mares. The
Scythians inserted a flute-shaped tube of bone into the
mare's genitals, and blew. While one Scythian blew, another milked. The blowing is said to have inflated the
mare's "veins" (uterus?), which then applied pressure on
the udder, facilitating the exit of milk. This is a fascinating technique,* but its connection with the blinding of
slaves was very oblique. The Scythians made the blind
men stand in a circle, pour the milk into wooden casks,
stir it, and skim off the cream. This is all Herodotus tells

---

* Carleton Coon says it is also practiced in Africa, by the Masai,
Bantu, and others.

us. The blind men were clearly connected with the milking process, but this does not explain why they were blinded. They could have been blindfolded. Unless the mares were always milked on the darkest nights it is hard to understand how blinding could have made these men better milk-skimmers. One can easily imagine them missing the wooden casks and pouring the milk on the ground. We are left in a quandary. But Herodotus then turns abruptly from this mare-milking diversion, and leaves us with a final clue to the Scythians' motives: "The reason why they blind their prisoners of war is connected with the fact that the Scythians are not an agricultural people, but nomadic."

That is all he says, but it does leave us with food for thought. The slaves were prisoners of war. We are expected to understand at once that nomadic people would blind their prisoners of war, apparently as a matter of course. Blind slaves would be more of a nuisance in a nomadic tribe than in a settled village (where they could gradually learn to feel their way around), which gives us cause to suspect that nomads may have had more reason to fear their enemies. If these enemies had been extremely ruthless, cruel — and dangerous — it may have been wise to take precautions against further acts of atrocity from those who were spared to help with the milking. Blind men may have been less adept not only at skimming milk, but also at slitting throats. In any case, there seems to have been a connection with warfare as well as with milking mares and the nomadic way of life.

If so, this could help to explain how otherwise affectionate people could blind their prisoners — or, indeed, how
their descendants could have built so many bombs.

The effect of foreign enemies on Scythian behavior becomes even more apparent when we consider some of the
other customs described by Herodotus. Not all prisoners
of war were blinded. Some were sacrificed to the Scythian god Ares. One man out of every hundred prisoners
had his throat cut over a bowl, and while the bowl of
blood was being carried to the top of a sacrificial wood-
pile, the other prisoners were slaughtered and their severed right arms and hands were thrown into the air. This
ceremony rendered harmless the bodies of the foreigners
who took part in it, even though their souls may have
gone marching on. The Scythians seem to have been
aware of possible hazards from such marching souls.
When certain chieftains died, they were not sent skulk-
ing alone into the spirit world. They rode boldly into
those regions that teemed with the revengeful souls of
their maimed and dismembered enemies — at the head
of a carefully chosen cavalry formation. Fifty of the
chief's best men were strangled, gutted, stuffed with
chaff, and sewn up again. Fifty of the finest horses received the same treatment. Wagon wheels were then cut
in half and fixed rim-downward to stakes driven into the
ground. Stout poles were then driven lengthwise, tail to
neck, through the stuffed horses, which were then
mounted on the wagon wheel supports — one just behind the forelegs, the other just before the hips — with
the hooves dangling clear of the ground. Poles were then

driven through the stuffed men, parallel with their spines, and the lower ends of these poles were fitted into sockets in the horse stakes. Each human corpse was thus mounted and ready for action on the carcass of a horse. When this frightful cavalry force was well in place around the chief's tomb, the mourners went away — possibly confident that the disembodied social group would be able to conquer and hold a corner of the spirit land. Concubines, cooks, butlers, and other servants were also strangled to ensure that the pleasures and comforts of the chief's decomposing body would not be neglected. The influence of foreign enemies on Scythian social behavior was thus extended to the grave, and beyond.

These burial customs were very fierce, very savage, and disturbingly like those of more recent ancestors — the Vikings, who sent their chiefs to Valhalla in battleships. We must remember, however, that the young Scythians who rode into the Great Unknown with their chieftain apparently accepted this grisly mission with stoic courage. This is one of the most difficult of all forms of social cooperation, and social cooperation is the most distinctive achievement of man. We must add this to the scales when we weigh the pros and cons of Scythian behavior.

According to Herodotus: "The Scythian custom is for every soldier to drink the blood of the first man he kills. The heads of all enemies killed in battle are taken to the king; a head being a sort of ticket by which the soldier is admitted to his share of the loot — no head, no loot."

Apart from their value as loot tickets, severed enemy

heads served other purposes. The soldiers skinned their enemies' heads by making a circular cut round the ears and shaking out the skull. The flesh was carefully scraped from the skin, which was then kneaded with the fingers until it was supple enough for use as a handkerchief. These hankies were hung from the bridle of the soldier's horse, and he was very proud of them. Herodotus says: "The finest fellow is the man who had the greatest number." Many Scythians sewed these scalps together and made cloaks of them, probably ranking each other thereafter by length of cloak, a habit that has persisted to this day at Oxford University. Other Scythians skinned the right arms and hands, nails and all, of their dead enemies — for use as quiver covers. Herodotus noted that "human skin is not only tough, but white, as white as almost any skin." He called this a "fact," apparently from first-hand experience, but he was not referring to Nubian skins. Sometimes the Scythians flayed out an entire body and stretched the skin on a wooden frame which they carried with them as they rode. Squeamish deployers of nuclear weapons today may find these customs revolting, but this may have been the very reason for their observance by our Scythian ancestors. People who lived in and around southern Russia may have been even more revolted than we are, especially if a brother's fingernails were tapping tirelessly on some nomadic quiver. The very thought of these leather-clad cavalrymen moving in one's direction may have elicited plans for emigration to Hungary, Germany, or Scandinavia. This was precisely what

the Scythians may have been driving at. They were probably trying to impress their foreign enemies.

Most of their enemies, however, were not very foreign.
Un-Scythian activity was very unpopular on the steppes
in those days. Even Darius cut his visit short. Herodotus
says they were "dead set against foreign ways, especially
against Greek ways." Most non-Scythians who were able
to fight their way into Europe — or into the cold northern forests of Russia — had probably done so. Those who
remained to threaten the Scythians were mainly Scythians. The Greeks who remained on the shores of the
Black Sea did what they could to please the nomads,
judging from the styles of the art objects they were making. Herodotus tells how the Scythians served wine to
their guests in the gilded skulls of their relatives, while
the host "tells the story of them: how they were once his
relatives and made war against him . . ." Some of the
Scythian fugitives to Europe, possibly including those
who were buried in northern Germany, may have had
very compelling reasons for leaving home.

This has been a very one-sided look at Scythian customs. We must remember that Herodotus may have
been as dead set against their ways as they were against
his. We are not told of the nights of gay Scythian cama-
raderie, when good fellows got together round the fire,
quaffing wine from gilded skulls, slapping knees, and
roaring with virile laughter until they had to reach for
their leathern hankies and wipe the happy tears from
their eyes. They were probably as loyal and trustworthy

to their friends as they were ferocious to their enemies —
or they would not have been so formidable in war. They
probably mixed each other's blood in skull cups and
drank it together in pledges of loyalty to the death, curs-
ing traitors as they did so. Many of them may have kept
these pledges as scrupulously as we now keep pledges to
defend our underdeveloped friends from our highly developed enemies. The Scythians were probably as warm
and friendly as we are, and if they clad themselves in human leather to impress their enemies — we must remember that deterrents are not effective unless they are
credible.

Scythian social habits differed in certain details from
those of other nomads, but the broad features were similar for at least two thousand years, from one end of the
steppes to the other. Horses were always valued very
highly, and there was always a keen awareness of danger
from foreign enemies. G. L. Seidler attributes these
words to Genghis Khan:

The greatest happiness for a man, and the greatest joy, is
to defeat and exterminate the enemy, to destroy him in his
very roots, to take all he possesses, to force his wives to weep,
to ride his best and beloved horses, and to have the joy of
possessing his beautiful women.

This may not be an exact translation of the words that
crossed the great Khan's lips, but the evidence of history
testifies that the idea was firmly established in his mind.

Since we are speaking here of Genghis Khan, it may be necessary to remind the reader that he was referring to his *enemies*, not to his very numerous friends. His words express in a nutshell the very essence of the forces that trebled the size of the human brain. The foremost aim of man has always been the survival of his friends and relations, and human enemies have always been the greatest threat to this survival. The winners of the struggle into manhood destroyed enemy *males* and sowed their *own* seed in conquered females. Success in these conquests was greatly favored by mobility, and so the horse was deeply loved by those who were not destroyed in their very roots on the Asian steppes. When we blame our ancestors for this savage approach to life, we blame them for our own birth. The survival of our species, *now*, depends on our ability to suppress the urge to kill our enemies, but we are not now living on the steppes of many years ago. Let us pause before we judge our ancestors by our own standards. Times have changed, and we must change, but let us not blame our ancestors for surviving. None of them survived for very long as individuals, and can we censure them for living long enough to bequeath the genes that produced our own hands and hearts and brains?

Genghis Khan was alive for only sixty-five years, but he achieved far more than his own brief survival during that short time. It is encouraging that we can recoil in horror from his wholesale extermination of untold millions, now that we are poised and ready for slaughter beyond the wildest dreams of Genghis Khan. But if we linger overlong in a warm illusion of our own self-righteousness, or concentrate *only* on the atrocities of the Mongols, we may fail to see that part of Genghis Khan which is most essential for the survival of our species.

Juvaini, who was born the year before the great Khan died, became the secretary of the founder of the Mongol dynasty of northern Persia. His father had also served the Mongols, and his grandfather had been a minister of the kings of Khiva, defeated opponents of Genghis Khan in the first invasion of the west. Juvaini had reason to say good things about the Mongols — just as we now have reason to utter pleasant sounds in the presence of those who can lock the doors of our ivory towers. But Juvaini, in the service of the Mongols, wrote accounts of their atrocities that few secretaries of today's political leaders would dare even to imply. He described the fate of Bamiyan as follows:

Chingiz-Khan gave orders that every living creature, from mankind down to the brute beasts, should be killed; that no prisoner should be taken; that not even the child in its mother's womb should be spared; and that henceforth no living creature should dwell therein . . . And to this very day no living creature has taken up abode therein.

Juvaini's *History of the World-Conqueror* groans with long accounts of brutal savagery. Page after page is filled with the grisly details. He cites a census of the dead at Merv which arrived at "a figure of more than one million three hundred thousand . . ." — not counting those killed later in holes, cavities, villages, and deserts. He describes the cold-blooded execution of the slaughter at Merv in these terms:

The Mongols now entered the town and drove all the inhabitants . . . out onto the plain. For four days and nights the people continued to come out of the town . . . The Mongols ordered that, apart from four hundred artisans whom they specified and selected from amongst the men and some children, girls and boys, whom they bore off into captivity, the whole population, including the women and children, should be killed, and no one, whether woman or man, be spared. The people of Merv were then distributed among the soldiers and levies, and, in short, to each man was allotted the execution of three or four hundred persons . . .

During a similar slaughter at Tirmiz, a woman is said to have told the Mongols that if they would spare her she would give them a great pearl. They asked where it was and she said she had swallowed it. "Whereupon they ripped open her belly and found several pearls. On this account Genghis Khan commanded that they should rip open the bellies of all the slain."

City after city received the treatment of Bamiyan, Merv, and Tirmiz — and Juvaini describes them all, sparing few details. The inhabitants of defeated towns and cities were not always massacred (this apparently depended on the degree of resistance offered). But some towns surrendered without a struggle, offering gifts and other tokens of supplication, and were exterminated nevertheless. Balkh was one of these. The Mongols had no confidence in their professions of submission and they were marched out onto the plain, divided as usual into hundreds and thousands, and put to the sword. At Nishapur the severed heads were stacked in piles, those of the men separate from those of the women and children. Juvaini neither omitted nor praised these gory details, and the Mongol ruler of northern Persia was looking over his shoulder as he wrote. The descendants of Genghis Khan may have been proud of their grandfather's atrocities, but they did not continue them. From the very start the Mongol aim had been more farsighted than mere annihilation — and this farsighted aim had been the very secret of their success. Juvaini tells us that:

. . . when Chingiz-Khan's cause prospered and the stars of his fortune were in the ascendant, he dispatched envoys to the other tribes also; and all that came to tender submission, such as the Oirat and the Quoqurat, were admitted to the number of his commanders and followers and were regarded with the eye of indulgence and favor; while as for the refractory and rebellious, he struck the breath from their bodies with the whip of calamity and the sword of annihilation; until all the tribes were of one color and obedient to his command. Then he established new laws and laid the foundation of justice; and whichever of their customs were abominable, such as theft and adultery, he abolished . . .

The Mongol tribes and clans learned law and order under Genghis Khan, but he did not have to teach them violence:

Before the appearance of Chingiz-Khan they had no chief or ruler. Each tribe or two tribes lived separately; they were not united with one another, and there was constant fighting and hostility between them.

At times Juvaini became quite carried away on the wings of his love for the Mongols:

When the hand of the creation of power had placed the signet of the Empire upon the finger of his fortune, he dispatched armies to all sides and every land, and most of the climes were purged of his adversaries. The fame of his justice and beneficence became an earring in all ears and his favors and kindnesses like bracelets on the hands and forearms of all. His Court became an asylum to all the world and his presence a refuge and shelter to the whole earth. As the lights of the dawn of his equity were without the dust of the darkness of evening, so the extent of his empire reached from farthest Chin and Machin to the uttermost districts of Syria. His bounty was general to all mankind, and waited not for month or year. His being and generosity were two coursers running neck and neck, and his nature and constancy twin sucklings at one breast . . . And in the prospect of his mercy and compassion hope revived in every breast. And such as had survived the sword remained in the noose of life and the bed of security.

Many men of today will be irked by Juvaini's exclusion of Europe from the world, and Europeans from mankind — but this may be because we were taught in school that Alexander the Great, and later the Romans, had conquered "the world." Juvaini's extravagant praise was not due *entirely* to the fact that he was in the employ of the Mongols. The very excesses of Genghis Khan had produced powerful surges of love in the hearts of many of those who had, miraculously, survived. After such convincing demonstrations of what happens to those who do not love the Khan, it is not surprising that many succeeded in finding, and then nurturing, a spark of love in their hearts. While they were surrounded and governed by Mongols it was not safe merely to *profess* one's love. The people of Balkh had tried this in vain. A mere mask over a deeper dislike for the Mongols might be a flimsy shield against the sword of the just and beneficent one. A mere word or a glance, at an unguarded moment, might be sufficient to reveal these inner feelings to the eye of an observant Mongol. It was far safer to *believe*, in one's inmost heart, that the Khan was the source of all tenderness and love and bounty and justice. Under such conditions real *faith* is sorely needed as a shield and buckler. Just as in the Europe of those same centuries it was safer to *believe* than to be boiled in oil, so was it in the empires of the great Khans. The only real difference was that social cohesion and religious freedom were far greater in Asia.

Is there no clue here to the origins of religious faith — or to the origin of the disciplined restraint required for large-scale civilization? Is it possible to subdue such an omnipresent chaos of petty warfare, as that between the vicious little city-states of ancient Greece, by philosophical discourse or by appeals to an illusion of man's Better

Nature? Can the ferocious turbulence of so many short-sighted savages be quelled and controlled by men who seek an answer to the blinding of prisoners of war in the milking of mares? Perhaps it is time to face up to the lesson of history and admit that confused multitudes will slaughter one another unless men of greater vision prevent them from doing so — by force if necessary. The violence in man *must* be deterred, and the deterrent must be credible — even to the simplest minds. We can learn a great deal from the history of Genghis Khan, which differs from the rest of history only in the swiftness and breadth of its sweep, and in the crystal clarity with which it reveals the simultaneous tragedy and glory of man.

The Mongol story can also tell us things about the flow of human genes. Juvaini says:

Chingiz-Khan had much issue, both male and female, by his wives and concubines. . . . And therefore he was wont to urge the strengthening of the edifice of concord and the consolidation of the foundations of affection between sons and brothers; and used continually to sow the seed of harmony and concord in the breasts of his sons and brothers and kinsfolk, and to paint in their hearts the picture of mutual aid and assistance. And by means of parables he would fortify that edifice and reinforce those foundations. One day he called his sons together and taking an arrow from his quiver he broke it in half. Then he took two arrows and broke them also. And he continued to add to the bundle until there were so many arrows that even the athletes were unable to break them. Then turning to his sons he said: "So it is with you also. A frail arrow, when it is multiplied and supported by its fellows, not even mighty warriors are able to break it, but in impotence withdraw their hands therefrom. As long, therefore, as you brothers support one another and render stout assistance one to another, though your enemies be men of great strength and might, yet shall they not gain victory over you."

Men had heard this story for thousands of years before Mongols were born, but few have understood its significance better than Genghis Khan.

According to Juvaini:

The children and grandchildren of Chingiz-Khan are more than ten thousand, each of whom has his own position, *yurt,* army and equipment. To record them all is impossible; our purpose in relating this much was to show the harmony which prevails among them as compared with what is related concerning other kings, how brother falls upon brother and son mediates the ruin of father till of necessity they are vanquished and conquered and their authority is downfallen and overthrown.

The achievement of human harmony seems to have had something to do with the spread of genes, and with changes in gene frequency — that is, with evolution.

SHIPS

Water has increased the rate of human motion, and hence of natural selection, for many millennia. Human civilization made its first little kicks against the womb of evolution along the banks of rivers. But the seas were not the element of man. The stillness of the ocean deep was not broken by the din of human warfare until very recent centuries. The seas remained a barrier as formidable as outer space itself until man learned how to build sea-worthy ships and how to guide them to his destination. He took a long time learning this. Even the courageous Carthaginian captains hugged the coast, looking out at the deep with misgiving. Greeks and Romans also cherished the sight of land, and no Chinese junks ever entered the harbors of Ostia, Carthage, or Athens. Apart from a few brief social exchanges with Vikings, the American Indians were left to scalp each other in peace until 1492. The seas were not the scene of human evolution.

However, men have been floating outward from the mouths of rivers for a long time — into the Mediterranean, the Persian Gulf, the Arabian and Yellow seas. Most of these men were not diffused over any great distances. No Egyptian colonies appeared in Spain, and the barnacles of the Arabian and Yellow seas were not greatly intermixed by the hulls of protohistoric ships. But there is evidence that men were moving along the coasts of Europe in boats as early as 2200 B.C. Geoffrey Bibby suggests that traders and missionaries sailed from Crete in these early days, weighed anchor in Denmark, and made the return trip of four thousand miles in the same ships. Julius Caesar was only dimly aware of Denmark when he invaded Britain, but Bibby assumes that, two thousand years earlier, his Cretan missionaries were much better informed. This evangelistic theory is one of many that have tried to explain an interesting trail of human relics along the seacoasts from Crete through Malta, Sicily, Italy, Sardinia, southern France and Spain, and up the western coast of Spain to Brittany, Ireland, Wales, and Denmark. Along this trail, a series of remarkable graves changes gradually from a vaulted, dry-stone structure in the south to a megalithic slab construction in the north. There seems to be a fascinating family likeness between all these graves, and as the archaeologists back-track from Denmark to Crete, the greater this likeness seems to become. Without debating Bibby's evangelistic interpretation, or the "prospector" theory, or other serene imaginings about those happy days of yore, it does seem that most archaeologists agree that some kind of movements were taking place by sea. Glyn Daniel speaks of "settlers" and "colonists," though he suggests that megalithic architecture may have been developed *independently* at several places in prehistoric Europe. Even if the "diffusion" was primarily supernatural, in the form of a Cretan religion, there must have been a movement of lowly bodies as well. Ideas travel in "muddy vestures of decay," like brains and boats. Bibby's Cretan missionaries would have had to *visit* Ireland and Denmark in order to infuse the spirit of their mother-goddess into the benighted heathens forcefully enough to convert them to the back-breaking practice of megalithic architecture. Daniel suggests that this fascinating puzzle has yet to be solved, which is probably one of the soundest of all the theories that have emerged from its study. No attempt will be made to solve it here, apart from suggesting that it might be approached from a less tranquil point of view.

The movements and motives of these early mariners are lost in prehistory, and in the minds of modern archaeologists. But not long after chariots first appeared in the Near East, "Peoples of the Sea" irrupted suddenly from the eastern shores of the Mediterranean — to baffle historians for the next three thousand years. The names applied to these diverse tribes by Egyptians and Hittites will probably continue to baffle us indefinitely, but the source of the Sea Peoples, and the motive force behind them, are already reasonably clear. Hordes of cavalry were in motion on the steppes, and when nomadic cavalry moved, other people moved — even through forests and over water.

During the Golden Age of Mycenae the inhabitants of Greece fought one another with chariots — but they also fought with ships. The coastal towns were heavily fortified. Egyptian and Cretan and Levantine objects in Mycenaean graves may have been acquired by piracy. We have no good reason to assume, with Alan Samuel, that *all* Mycenaean swords brought money instead of blood. Given only that they fought by sea as well as by land, it is easy to understand how natural selection could have been swift and savage in the Aegean during the second millennium B.C. If so, it is not surprising that primitive indications of civilization on the continent of Europe appeared first in Greece.

The diffusion of Greeks to Sicily and Italy and the Crimea followed sea-lanes — hugging the coast, to be sure, but moving by sea. We know they fought each other as they expanded, and pushed less mobile people back from the coasts. Although they did not establish themselves in numbers very far inland, they were lively disturbers of the peace along the shores. Another people also began to sail the waters of the Mediterranean at the same time — the Phoenicians. These Phoenicians appeared a few centuries after Sea Peoples had hacked out homes for themselves along the coasts of Palestine. The Philistines, who shared such lively social get-togethers with King David's Israelites, carried "Sea People" genes. They were mainly Semitic, but partly Indo-European.* When they founded colonies at Carthage and elsewhere, they took care to select defensible islands and peninsulas. Neither the sea nor the land was immune from the forces of natural selection. Gradually, the Greeks and Phoenicians transformed the Mediterranean from a vast barrier into a great highway.

In the meantime, natural selection was proceeding energetically on land, particularly in Italy. Around 2000 B.C., when chariots were appearing in Mesopotamia, Indo-European-speaking tribesmen poured into Italy from the north and spread southward over the peninsula. While the Greeks and Phoenicians were cutting out "clearings" around certain harbors, Etruscans, Latins, Sabines, Umbrians, Samnites, Lucanians, and other lesser folk were chopping busily at one another in Italy. The forests and

---

* Those who refuse to use the term *Indo-European* in an ethnic sense may wish to substitute the word *Aryan* here.

mountains stood in their way, blocking their little armies here and there, but they moved around and through these obstacles with surprising speed. By 400 B.C. the pace of movement was even livelier. Aequi, Volsci, Gauls, and many others joined in the fray. Despite forests and rivers and mountains alike, Celtic Gauls swept south from the Po to Rome and then back again, laden with loot and undefeated. Celts were in contact with leather-clad Scythians, and many of them may have been descended (in part) from Cimmerians and Scythians. The Latins, Sabines, and others may also have carried genes that had flowed westward from the steppes. Mobility had come to Italy. The pace of action quickened. Gradually the Romans conquered Samnites, Marsi, Vestini, Paeligni, Frentani, Apulians, Ausones, Lucanians, Marrucini, Sallentini and Hernicans. They not only conquered them, but also welded them into the lusty youth of a powerful social organization. Then the young social giant looked seaward for bigger game.

Galleys and galley slaves grew in number, until finally Carthage was exterminated and the Mediterranean became a Roman lake. Without this sea — this relatively *calm* sea — the great Roman Empire could not have been founded, or held together. The sea was becoming a factor in human evolution. But the great beating heart of human evolution was still pumping away in central Asia, sending genes under pressure along arteries that led into China and India and Hungary — and even to the finest capillaries in Scandinavia and Britain. These great pressures were to swamp the empire of Rome, and to send genes *overland*, even through Spain, across the Straits of Gibraltar, and *overland* again along the northern coast of Africa. The genes from the steppes would not begin to flow in great volume over the seas until a thousand years after Rome collapsed.

But once the great sea-flow began, it was to become an enormous tidal wave of change that would swell the affairs of men to global dimensions. Dutchmen and Portugese would appear on the shores of India and Borneo. Spanish conquistadores would alter the course of evolution in Mexico and Peru. The sea would recoil from the shock of broadsides. The Jolly Roger would snap in the winds of the Spanish Main. Legs and masts would be blasted off at Trafalgar, and the sun would fail to set on British soil. A great flood of genes would roll from Europe and Africa into the Americas. Tribes would be annihilated in Australia and Tasmania, and caucasoid genes would flow north from the southernmost tip of Africa. The great steppes themselves would be surrounded by their own spawn of genes. Russia would send long tentacles eastward to Alaska, seeking an ice-free outlet to the new highway. China would finally turn from her Wall to meet invasion from Japan. Bombs would shake the very center of the vast Pacific, and an American flag would be raised on Iwo Jima. This colossal change cannot be traced to any single source, but its keel was laid in Scandinavia.

The North Atlantic has no sympathy for ships. Even the *Titanic* was drawn, without a qualm, beneath its heaving surface. Small open craft of wood cannot cross this wilderness of water unless they are built with the greatest skill and foresight. They must yield to the stress of heavy seas, and then regain their shape without breaking. They must be resilient and flexible, and yet they must cling to the curved lines of the form that holds them poised and upright on the turbulent and undulating surface. Their weight must not submerge them, even when they fall unrestrained from the highest crest to the deepest trough. One single failure can destroy them. They must hold their course through fog and sleet and rain. They must be controlled by men who remain undaunted by the icy ruthlessness supporting and surrounding them — from horizon to horizon, and beyond.

Such men, and such ships, emerged from Scandinavia. Like the Huns and the Mongols, they emerged as a Scourge of God in the eyes of other men, but they began to transform the Seven Seas into a single link between all continents, and thus between all men. Only one other people conquered the ocean deeps with less help — the Polynesians of the South Pacific. But the Polynesians weighed anchor centuries late. They diffused into the trackless wastes of the vast Pacific rather than into the turbulent wreckage of Rome, and their ingenious canoes would not have been a good prototype for the massive hulls of Captain Cook's *Resolution* and *Discovery*. Their experiment on the sea, like those of the Aztecs and Incas on land, was abruptly swamped by the tide from Europe. The "port" side of modern ships is on the left (when one is facing forward). There is no particular reason for modern ships to place this port side against the wharf while receiving or yielding cargo — but there was a very good reason for Viking ships to do so. The steering board, or rudder, of Viking ships was on the right, or "starboard" side; it was a massive oar-blade strapped to the *outer* side of the starboard gunwale — and so it was wise to keep this side away from the wharf. Our modern terminology has evolved from this right-handed Viking tradition.

The ships of the Vikings sailed not only across the North Sea, and to America, but also up shallow rivers, to the very heart of England and Europe. The Gokstad ship was 76½ feet long, but she drew only three feet in the water. These long, graceful agents of natural selection slid quietly over shallow sheets of water during the night, and waited silently for the dawn beside sleeping villages. For three hundred years they carried blades that drew thousands of gallons of blood from the hearts of Europe. They reached Gibraltar, slipped past the Pillars of Hercules, and infested the Mediterranean. They floated down the Dnieper, crossed the Black Sea, and appeared in force at the walls of Byzantium — from which they withdrew, laden with "tribute." The men of Europe were strong, and very savage. They had survived the frightful carnage that preceded and followed Attila the Hun. They vastly outnumbered the Vikings, and were a match for them — man for man. But they were sluggish and the Vikings were incredibly mobile. The longships came suddenly out of the dawn, and before the little armies of Europe arrived they were gone, leaving the would-be avengers to wander in impotence through the smoking ruins, slipping on the blood. The continent lay defenseless, like a great wounded beast, her very veins and arteries exposed to the keels and scalpels of the Vikings. Europe fell to her knees and prayed: "A *furore Normannorum libera nos.*"

The Viking ship did not appear as a sudden flash of inspiration in the mind of any single man. It evolved slowly, for many centuries, among the multitudinous islands, rivers, and fjords of Scandinavia. Like the brains that conceived and fashioned it, the Viking ship was bought with human blood. The mobile men survived, while the blood of those who built inferior ships dissolved in the water of the fjords, or congealed in the icy deeps offshore. Long before the entire continent of Europe cried for mercy, the furies of Scandinavia had been very active locally. Just as the Huns and Mongols had been absorbing their own arrows before they produced Attila and Genghis Khan, so had the Vikings been culling each other before they gave birth to Swegn Forkbeard, Canute, and William the Conqueror. When they emerged to feed like a swarm of sharks on the crippled and ponderous bulk of Europe, they were fighting one another with desperate savagery. Winston Churchill says they cooked their feasts of victory in caldrons hung on spits that pierced the bodies of their defeated enemies. After a battle in Ireland between Norwegians and Danes, the local Irish inhabitants (described by Churchill as "none too particular") expressed horror at this frightful habit — and asked the celebrating Vikings why they did it. They were told: "Why not? They would do it to us if they won." It is said that, during their winter feasts, the Vikings drank ale from the skulls of their defeated enemies — a custom reminiscent of our death-defying Scythian ancestors.

When Harald Fairhair imposed his *Pax* on Norway he sent a swarm of his Norwegian enemies coursing outward to England, Ireland, Iceland, and eventually to far-off Greenland. More than one fleet of Viking raiders sailed *eastward*, from England to Norway, seeking revenge from those who had driven them out of their native land. King Harald's son and first successor, Erik Bloody-Axe, received his nickname for applying his axe to the skulls of some of his numerous brothers. Erik was driven from Norway by a younger brother, Haakon the Good, who sailed from *England*. Erik was finally killed in England, not Norway. The traffic between England and Scandinavia was not all one-way during the Viking Age. The pressures that sent the Vikings swarming out to rend and tear the flanks of Europe, and the very heart of Russia, were many and varied. But they cannot be described adequately as a boyish "spirit of adventure" or "trade." Their swords brought blood as well as danegeld, and their bodies brought genes as well as terror to England, Ireland, Normandy, Sicily, Russia, and Iceland. Scandinavia was never a hot center on a scale approaching that of central Asia — but it was nevertheless a source of very lively-deadly social life for several centuries, and the speed of action was greatly accelerated by ships. Mobility — on land or sea — has had a very powerful effect on human evolution. The explosion from Scandinavia subsided, following the age-old pattern of history — but then the entire western half of Europe exploded into the seas, and men on every continent prayed for deliverance.

The foundations of global cooperation were not laid gently by philosophers who dreamed wistfully of Prehistoric Peace. They were laid brutally by men who sought power and *Lebensraum* — but like the keels of Viking ships, they were laid well. We now have the power to establish a global *Pax*, and we may even have brains enough to maintain a just and enduring one.

VII

PREHISTORIC PEACE

A FORCE THAT KILLS can be a factor in evolution. Even a very weak selective force can be effective if it persists. The removal by predators of only a few baboons each year has important evolutionary results, and for at least five thousand years, warfare has killed far more than a few humans. Why, then, has it been almost completely ignored in so many recent books, articles, and symposia on human evolution? Are all these authorities convinced that peace was absolute and eternal throughout the entire two or three million years of human prehistory? It would seem so, for they all know that even a slight selective force can have an important effect on evolution. The editors of *Life*, in their *Epic of Man*, have informed the general public that warfare began in the cities of Sumer only a few thousand years ago. With very few exceptions, this is the assumption of our modern authorities. It is a very sweeping assumption indeed, and it contradicts an enormous body of historical evidence. We might expect, therefore, that it is based on an even more enormous, and more convincing, volume of actual evidence of prehistoric peace. But prehistoric peace is very rarely supported with evidence. It is merely taken for granted. Gordon Childe and Carleton Coon both say that prehistoric men probably engaged one another in mortal combat, but most modern authorities convey an impression of almost idyllic prehistoric peace.

In a book called *Four Thousand Years Ago*, Geoffrey Bibby follows the sun around the earth, describing the birth of the second millennium B.C. As the mists of the third millennium dissolve in the growing light, a gentle panorama of childish peace unfolds before our eyes. The sleepy Egyptian who steps from his doorway has *heard* of war (his legends tell of Falcon Kings and Conquest) but he knows little of this, and cares less; he has even heard of raids into the delta during the past year or two, but this too is far away and in the background of his mind. In Mesopotamia a small band of workmen have heard of Sargon the Great, who died nearly three hundred years ago, and they are sufficiently aware of the threatening Elamites and Amorites east and west of them to keep their bronze-tipped spears ready to hand. There is a hint of latent violence in this semicivilized dawn, but a capitalist revolution is under way, replacing the older, communist form of administration, and the future holds great promise. In the Indus valley "Mongols," negroid Dravidians,* and beak-nosed Armenoids mingle amicably in the broad streets, trading cloth and oil and flour.

---

* Bibby describes these Dravidians as "dark, almost negroid," but Carleton Coon says that insofar as they were not caucasoid, Dravidians were australoid, not negroid.

These are the semicivilized regions, where war has begun to appear on the human scene, but even here men are mercifully unaware of the savage furies the second millennium holds in store.

In the backwoods of Scandinavia the natives have been friendly for generations, and the night watch has merely been a precaution against wolves and bobcats. Many travelers from faraway lands are welcomed hospitably by these genial Scandinavians, and the berserk Viking Age is still nearly three thousand years away. In the milder lands of southern England, life is good; the earth ramparts on Windmill Hill are calm and peaceful; only twice each year do they echo to the gay shouts and laughter of the herdsmen. A feeling of relationship, of belonging together, holds all the peoples of western Europe in a tenuous but warm sense of blood brotherhood. Like the morning mists, the Brotherhood of Man has not quite disappeared from these sylvan glades, and the trenches have yet to be dug along the western front. In the extreme south of Spain the towns are fortified with wall and ditch, but the sleepy townsmen are not expecting war; they look forward rather to giving the fruits of their civilization to the benighted barbarians north and west of them.

In Africa, dark-skinned farmers know warlike contact with Egypt, but those who live far from the corrupting influence of civilization have based their lives on agriculture and hunting, not on war. These people have songs and legends and village councils; Bibby reminds us that we mustn't assume they know nothing of themselves, merely because *we* know nothing of them. In China the backward farmers are quite unaware of Bibby's suggestion that the idea of agriculture has come to them from the west, moving slowly from oasis to oasis across the vast expanse of central Asia. As the first light falls on the second millennium B.C., these remote ancestors of modern China are secure in the illusion that their own forefathers arrived at the idea of agriculture on their own, unprompted by foreigners living thousands of miles to the west.

In Peru the villagers sit on their own refuse, eating mussels and adding the shells to the growing heap. They wear colorful shawls and are unconcerned about their ignorance of pottery, for they are the most advanced people in the world, so far as they know, "and they have reason to be proud of the fact." In South Africa the Bushmen are already on the trail of their quarry, pouncing on lizards and grubbing tubers as they go. Other hunting and gathering peoples (like the Bushmen in culture, if not in form and features) have also found the spoors of their quarry as the growing light returns to the Congo, the Amazon, Australia, and Siberia. These hunting and gathering peoples are more remote from warfare than were even our genial Scandinavians — and war lies not behind them in the past, but before them in the remote future. It will not reach them until civilization finds them; only then will they know the savage insanity of bloodstained battlefields. In the meantime they will be much too busy gathering and hunting, for food is scarce and hard to get; starvation is never far away and they never squabble over food, land, or women — certainly not in a way that modern men would dignify by calling it war. Like the beasts that surround them, these simple children of nature are innocent; they have yet to taste the apple of good and evil — Us and Them.

In the mists of Bibby's peaceful dawn it is not easy to find the prototypes of the warriors who are to rend and tear each other's flesh throughout the second millennium B.C. This terrible storm will break without warning. Bibby's dawn provides scant grounds for predicting that Joshua will be commanded by his Yahweh to kill all who breathe in the cities that worship other gods in the Promised Land. If we accept the vision of primitive peace that our scholars unfold before us, we must be forgiven if we fail to understand the apparent depravity of civilized man.

In 1964 Bertram S. Kraus made this remarkable statement:

The acquisition of the upright posture rendered this Primate *hors de combat*. He was shorn of the weapons, agility, speed, acuity of senses, and bodily protection which had hitherto allowed him to compete successfully with other members of the Animal Kingdom and to adapt to his total environment. No longer could he withstand the direct forces of the natural environment. The equipment so carefully developed over hundreds of millions of years of evolutionary selection was "suddenly" stripped from him.

We do not yet understand many features of the evolutionary process, but the vast bulk of the evidence we have suggests that no such "sudden" increase in helplessness could ever have occurred. What we know of evolution suggests that the erect posture conferred *more* rather than less capacity for defense, throughout every stage of its evolution. Darwin's suggestion that weapon use may have been involved is far more plausible than the *hors de combat* idea. The ancestors of early man were living on the African savanna, and perhaps in other unsympathetic environments.

Desmond Morris put the *hors de combat* point of view like this:

To start with, he had the wrong kind of sensory equipment for life on the ground. His nose was too weak and his ears not sharp enough. His physique was hopelessly inadequate for arduous endurance tests and for lightning sprints. In personality he was more competitive than cooperative and no doubt poor on planning and concentration. But fortunately he had an excellent brain, already better in terms of general intelligence than that of his carnivore rivals. By bringing his body up into a vertical position, modifying his hands in one way and his feet in another, and by improving his brain still further and using it as hard as he could, he stood a chance.

If we use our brains as hard as we can we might be able to see why this idea is far more *hors de combat* than our ancestors ever were, but we will not enlarge or improve the actual physical construction of our brains merely by doing this. Evolution is a result of natural selection, not of wishful thinking.

Anthropologists enjoy speculation — provided it

doesn't disturb their prehistoric peace. A recent collection of articles on the social life of early man was reviewed by Wilson Wallis* as follows: "Most of the implications are unwarranted, many are indefensible, some are as pure fiction as a biography of the man-in-the-moon."

With such strong leanings toward speculation, it is strange that there has been so little on the possibility of prehistoric *warfare*. There is no dearth of evidence upon which it could be based. For example, Georges Roux reports that Kathleen Kenyon unearthed a remarkable settlement at Jericho, surrounded by a strong city wall of undressed stone which has been radiocarbon-dated at 6800 B.C. The wall was built almost nine thousand years ago. Would the descendants of men who had survived for millions of years without stone wall defenses have built it for protection from lions? Did they build it for exercise? Or did they build it for protection from the one distinctively warlike animal species?

According to the prehistoric peace doctrine, Australian aborigines should have been living in peace before the Europeans arrived. Carleton Coon says they represent the survival, with very little change, of a cultural level found elsewhere between 70,000 and 100,000 years ago, and that they were not, and are not, peaceful. Russel Ward, however, describes them — under the heading "Mild Aborigines" — as the most primitive and peaceable peoples known to history. This judgment, of course, is relative. In the eyes of men who think in terms of total retaliation, the aborigines are peaceful in comparison.

* *Quarterly Review of Biology,* vol. 38 (1963), pp. 219–220.

But they were not always mild in their dealings with other aborigines. Gnawing at another man's throat until he is dead is neither a mild nor a peaceful form of behavior. Mothers taught their sons from infancy to watch and imitate the warriors.

New Guinea is another region that has only recently begun to feel the impact of the vices of civilization. By the mid–nineteenth century, even the coastal tribes had felt little contact with outside culture. Maslyn Williams says that, in 1964, only a few New Guinea natives were more than vaguely aware of a world outside. "There are many more," he says, "by thousands upon tens of thousands, to whom the outside world is less than a myth and its ways utterly inconsequential." He describes a small party of men from the interior being escorted by a government officer through a small frontier town, huddled closely together and looking about them fearfully, "their fingers feeling instinctively for the axes which they normally carry in their bark belts. For where these people live a stranger is an enemy, and death is the immediate and expected end of trespass."

These examples do not support the doctrine of prehistoric peace, and very few authorities have defended it with evidence. Back in the 1930's, however, Elliot Smith made a commendable effort to do this in a series of detailed descriptions of the behavior of more than twenty groups of living peoples who were at, or only just beyond, the food-gathering stage. His survey led him to this conclusion: "So long as he is free from the disturbing influence of civilization the nomad is by nature a happy and well-behaved child, full of generous impulses and free from vice."

Although they would not state it in these exact words, most modern authorities seem to agree with Smith's general view that primitive men were by nature peaceful. His evidence seems to have been almost unanimously accepted. To my knowledge, this view has not been supported by any more convincing evidence, yet attempts to refute it are very rare in the modern literature.

Smith believed, with the zeal of a missionary, in the sinfulness of civilized man and in the vice-free nature of primitive "children." His faith was so strong, in fact, that he arrived at this conclusion *despite* his own recorded evidence of warlike behavior in the Congo Pygmies, South African Bushmen, Andaman Islanders, Punan and allied tribes of Borneo, Australian aborigines, Eskimos, California Indians, and natives of Tierra del Fuego. These are the very peoples most often held up as "proof" of the mildness of prehistoric man, but Smith was not deterred by their warlike behavior. He attributed this to corrupting influences from civilized men.

He cites many examples of the "innocence" of primitive men. The Salish Indians of British Columbia, for example, are described in these words: "What is most pleasing to the stranger is to see their simplicity, united with sweetness and innocence, keep step with the most perfect dignity and modesty of deportment."

The Paiute of Nevada are another tribe cited by Smith as proof of primitive peacefulness. He said they were peaceful "as a rule," and though they were "not so bright in intellect" as the prairie tribes, they displayed more "solidity of character" in resisting the "vices of civilization."

The Punan of Borneo evoke idylls of morality and peacefulness. Smith referred to an account of them by Professor M'Dougall [sic] as "one of the most charming pictures ever drawn of the uncivilized peoples of the world." They lived in Central Borneo, surrounded by notorious headhunters who dominated the more favorable sites on the river banks. The Punan wandered peacefully through the forests without crops or domestic animals. Smith quotes a description of the behavior of the Punan in the presence of more warlike men:

> When gathered in friendly talk with strangers, even those whom they have every reason to trust, they prefer to remain squatting on their heels, rather than to sit down on a mat; and the tension of their muscles, combined with the still, alert watchfulness of their faces, conveys the impression that they are ready to leap up and flee away or to struggle for their lives at any moment. It is doubtless this alertness of facial expression and bodily attitude that gives the Punan something of the air of an untameable wild animal.

Such behavior is not surprising in people who are trying to live peacefully in the hunting grounds of headhunters, without losing their heads. Most civilized men would take small pride in descent from ancestors like the Punan, and such people will probably make a very modest contribution to the future gene pool of *Homo sapiens*.

These peaceful peoples were not as nonviolent as Smith's accounts might lead us to believe. It is perhaps fortunate that he was unaware of the arrows, poisoned with rattlesnake venom, that were carried in special dog-skin quivers by the Salish Indians — who reserved them for purposes other than hunting. Douglas Leechman says this technique was unusual for Canadian Indians, which suggests that the Salish people had worked it out for themselves, possibly while their sweetness and innocence were being given a rest. The Salish Indians were only one of several preagricultural tribes living in the British Columbia interior. If the preagricultural way of life is conducive to peaceful behavior, we should expect such behavior in *all* these tribes. The prehistoric-peace hypothesis assumes that peace prevailed for at least a million years between all humans everywhere; violent intergroup competition is excluded *wholesale* as a possible factor in human evolution. Such a sweeping hypothesis cannot be proved by selecting *apparently* peaceful groups out of a great mass of contrary evidence. Smith ignored the rest of the Indians who were living near the Salish tribe, and at the same cultural level. When we consider the behavior of these other tribes it is easy to understand why the Salish Indians dipped their arrows in rattlesnake venom.

Leechman says there was no agriculture of any kind in any of these tribes, apart from a little tobacco-growing by the Kootenays, and tobacco is not a food. He says there was little systematic warfare between them, though some fought each other more than others did. The Chilcotin often fought the Shuswap, the Kootenays had frequent trouble with the Blackfoot, while Smith's Salish tribe dipped their arrows. Many tribes occasionally raided other villages, for revenge or for slaves. Blood feuds occasionally escalated into small wars. Scalping was not usual, but special weapons were built for war rather than for hunting. One of these took the form of a stone lashed to the end of a club by a leather thong; Leechman says it was effective when under control, but risky to the user if he lacked experience. It is interesting to note that even such a primitive weapon can be risky to the user, though not in a thermonuclear way. It is also interesting to note that such wooden clubs, had they been used for war during the Pleistocene, would have long since decayed, and that the stones may have escaped the intelligent notice of archaeologists. According to Leechman, a favorite war tactic of these people was to pile logs and rocks on a mountainside, and then to roll them down on an enemy who was picking his way carefully along the narrow and difficult track below. Such logs and stones, had they been used in the same way during the Pleistocene, would no longer be recognizable as weapons of war by modern archaeologists. Leechman says that night raids on sleeping villages were also popular among these tribes. They were scattered widely in small hunting and gathering bands, and Leechman says they had a less exciting social life than the Iroquois (which may have been a blessing when we recall the Iroquois torture ceremonies). These widely scattered bands, however, seem to have devised exciting social interactions of their own. A night raid on a sleeping village can be very exciting indeed, both for the raiders and the raided. One social event of this kind each year could have provided sufficient excitement to last the survivors for at least six months, and would have given them something to look forward to for the remaining six. It is highly significant that these bands were widely dispersed, preagricultural, and not unaccustomed to war. Their little wars were not on the scale of Caesar's conquest of Gaul, but they should not be ignored as a possible evolutionary force.

Smith cites also the northern Ojibways (Chippewas) as an example of the peacefulness of primitive man. Leechman says there was no "organized" warfare among these people, but that friction between them was so constant that they might easily decide it was safer to kill strangers then to risk being killed themselves. This may be called self-defense rather than warfare, but it has evolutionary effects nevertheless.

According to Leechman, there was occasional trouble with the Eskimos; the Chippewas bullied the Dogribs and the Yellowknives; the Crees bullied the Chippewas; and they all felt it was safe to attack the "timid" Hares and Slaves. Oliver La Farge says the Chippewas forced the Sioux tribes westward, which could not have been easy. The pattern in northeastern North America, then, among the least agricultural tribes, was similar to that in the British Columbia interior, and another of Elliot Smith's allegedly peaceful peoples must be raised, or lowered, to the level of the rest of us.

The Paiute of Nevada were praised by Smith for resisting "the vices of civilization," but they were probably faced with temptation only rarely. They lived in desert country that offered scant facility for civilized vices. La Farge says they hunted prairie dogs, gophers, and rabbits, and were not above mice and grasshoppers. They took what the land had to offer, and according to La Farge, this included scalps. He says they did not fight often because they were too busy keeping themselves alive. When they were forced to fight, he says, they fought well, with effective bows, and with spears twelve feet long. Their military prowess was not, however, highly honored by their neighbors, and in some of the more warlike tribes the name *Paiute* came to mean "ignorance." This pathetically impoverished people stayed where they were — in the desert — with scarcely any social organization, because they were, according to La Farge, too few, too weak, and too poor to encroach on the more desirable lands of the more powerful tribes around them. Despite whatever "innate" equality they may have shared with nearby tribes, the Paiute, like the Kalahari Bushmen, failed to realize it.

The Punan of Borneo, like the Paiute of Nevada, seem to have been peaceful through sheer force of circumstances rather than "by nature." Smith concedes that they would fight back if attacked, when there was "no choice of flight." If a relative was murdered, they would seek an opportunity of planting a poisoned dart in the body of the murderer. But, like the Paiute, they could not compete with the military organizations of the surrounding tribes. Their peacefulness, then, was like that of modern prisoners of war — or that of the Australian aborigines who stood with only boomerangs and spears in their hands before the Europeans.

At any one time during the Pleistocene there must have been many scattered groups of people who, like the Paiute, the Bushmen, the Congo Pygmies, and today's Australian aborigines, were hovering on the brink of extinction in unwanted deserts, jungles, and cold northern forests. As the centuries succeeded one another, such peripheral peoples must often have passed into extinction, to be replaced by other fugitives from "hot centers." Some of the banished groups may have had great genetic potential for learning social organization, but the acid test has always been the actual *achievement* of such organization. The Paiute of Nevada may have been an exception to the general rule; Smith may have misjudged them when he said they were intellectually inferior. They may have been superior, genetically, but through some religious or political accident they may have clung too tenaciously to a tradition of rugged individualism. If so, good genetic material may have been squandered. In most cases, however, the people banished to the deserts would have been too "retarded" to learn social cooperation adequate for the defense or conquest of a more desirable area.

Several of Smith's allegedly peaceful peoples, such as the Punan, were not really living under preagricultural conditions. They were in close contact with agricultural peoples, and were therefore unsuitable as examples of human reactions to an early Stone Age environment. The Veddas of Ceylon, two Malayan tribes, a Sumatra tribe, New Guinea and Philippines tribes, were all cited by Smith as examples of the mildness of primitive man. All these peoples were surrounded by warlike agricultural peoples, and their "peacefulness" was imposed on them by force. If they are excluded as a likely source of evidence bearing on human social reactions in a prehistoric environment, Smith's roster of "primitive" peoples is left with the Lapps, Samoyeds, and Ostiaks, which he lumped as "Siberians." "Siberians" lived near the homelands of Huns, Mongols, Russians, and other mobile warriors, and it is clear from Russian history that they did not always greet invaders with open arms or bowed heads. A similar physical environment, in northern Canada, has also failed to ensure purely peaceful social interactions. The behavior of people under such conditions today cannot be regarded as representative of human behavior everywhere during the Pleistocene, but it still shows clearly that warfare takes place between preagricultural groups, even where population densities are very low.

Elliott Smith contends that primitive "children" do not fight "by nature." They do so only when threatened by other men. This is not a peculiarity of primitive men — it is what we all do. Highly civilized men can live in huge, congested cities without constantly seeking each other's heads as trophies, and without continually threatening to spear one another. If threatened, or if they imagine themselves threatened, civilized men can fight with very destructive weapons, but they do not do this for mere sport, or to release an "innate" and uncontrollable urge. Many an English soldier has envied gentlemen in England then abed, on the eve of the battle in which he was killed.

Smith could have found more convincing evidence of "peacefulness unless disturbed by the influence of civilization" in Sweden. Sweden has refrained from warfare *despite* civilized influences that must have been very disturbing indeed. Surely this is more commendable than peacefulness due merely to lack of provocation.

Smith concluded that the contented mind is the "divine gift," that the society in which all is peace is the healthy society, and that the standard of behavior of human society is a state of happy, stable cheerfulness, lacking in violence. His relegation of the contented mind to the realm of the supernatural is not a biological conclusion, nor a scientific one. His standard of behavior is an ethical conclusion, and though it is not the purpose of this book to debate ethics, the widespread belief in prehistoric peace has grown from ethical rather than rational roots, whether our leading anthropologists are aware of it or not. Smith's contented state of happy peace might be desirable to many people, but he does not explain how to achieve it. His revulsion from the trend towards centralization and megalopolises is shared by Aldous Huxley and Lewis Mumford, who advocate a return to autonomy within decentralized groups. However, our historical records and the anthropological studies of today's primitive people suggest that this cure for the ills of civilization might be worse than the disease.

Ashley Montagu believes in the peacefulness of primitive men with a missionary zeal as fervid as Elliot Smith's. He warns that we are in great danger today because we are beset by myths, one of the most insidious of which is the belief that our susceptibility to warfare is "innate." Few reasonable people would dispute the view that we are beset by myths. ("Other people" often seem to be particularly bedeviled in this way.) Primitive myths were the attempts of primitive men to explain natural phenomena which they could not understand. These attempts were almost always based on supernatural assumptions. We are still attempting to explain phenomena that we do not understand, and we still tend to invoke the supernatural occasionally. For example, we do not yet understand what, exactly, is "innate" in human behavior.

The words *innate* and *instinct* have been a source of confusion for a very long time. Dictionaries define them as synonymous with *inborn* or *natural*. Instinct is defined as an "innate" propensity to seemingly rational acts in both man and "lower" animals, or to actions that are essential to their existence, preservation, and development. In the older psychology, instincts were considered as chains of reflexes, or "inborn tendencies." Instinct is often considered also in terms of "intuition"; it usually implies an "animation from within," an "inward impulse," or a "spontaneous" and more or less "automatic" reaction. It is not always easy to prevent such concepts from getting tangled up with the supernatural. We are still very primitive, despite our nuclear weapons.

Scientists are trying to explain animal behavior in natural terms, and some of them are still trying to distinguish between "intelligent" and "instinctive" behavior. Birds, for example, build nests. They will do this without any previous training, and we can easily tell from a glance at a nest the species of bird that built it. Their behavior pattern has obviously been "bred into" them; it is "natural" and "innate." This is a clear case of instinctive behavior in the popular sense. It is not always easy, however, to distinguish between the "innate" and the "intelligent" elements of *mammalian* behavior. Nearly all of the more complex behavior of mammals is an intimate mixture of unlearned instincts and learned (intelligent) variations of the instinctive "theme." A bitch may suppress an instinctive urge to growl at the hand that has taught her obedience, when that hand moves toward one of her puppies. Any attempt to untangle the learned and unlearned elements of such behavior on an either-or basis will divert attention from the fact that most mammalian behavior is an intimate combination of the two. Carleton Coon (1963, p. 123) points out that although we really are born with built-in drives, many of them are uncoordinated at birth; both chimps and men, for example, must be taught how to copulate. Some scientists draw still another distinction, which tends to dissociate the components of human behavior still further. Lancelot Law White, for example, draws a distinction between "animal instinct," "animal intelligence," and "human intellect." The nest-building behavior of the bird would be an example of nearly pure animal instinct, the restraint of the dog an example of animal intelligence, and the language of humans an example of human intellect.

We like to exaggerate our superiority over other animals by assuming that we alone can think in terms of such symbols as "words," forgetting that other animals can also respond to mere symbols, and can associate the sound of a *particular* automobile, for example, with the probability of a *future* plateful of dogfood.* We like to think that we alone are able to anticipate the future, and we are often reluctant to concede that other animals may, in their humble way, share this capacity with us.

In his attempt to refute the myth that our susceptibility to warfare is innate (in the archaic sense) Montagu asserts that "savages" are not warlike, because they can "work themselves up to fighting pitch" only with difficulty. This implies that if warlike behavior *was* innate, these "savages" would carry it out with something like the clockwork precision of a bird building a nest. Montagu, Elliot Smith, Havelock Ellis, and others assert or imply that peaceful behavior *is* innate. They relegate peaceful behavior to the "instinctive," "unlearned" level of lower animals — and simultaneously elevate warlike behavior to the higher levels of human culture. According to this line of reasoning, "savages" are scarcely human at all. They are peaceful only blindly and auto-

* Similarities between human and subhuman brain processes are not easily understood if the alleged distinction between "signs" and "symbols" is accepted uncritically.

matically, and they can learn the distinctively human, warlike behavior only with difficulty.

Robert Ardrey argues that the Tierra del Fuegians, for example, were banished to that inhospitable region because they were too "timid" to resist the attacks of fiercer men. This argument implies that warlike behavior *is* unlearned and innate in the archaic sense. This is implied in the very title of Ardrey's recent book: *The Territorial Imperative*. Ardrey overlooks the possibility that the Tierra del Fuegians were banished from more fertile regions not because of their individual timidity, but because of their failure to *cooperate* in large enough numbers to repel armies larger than their own. However courageous or ferocious a lion, a gorilla, or an australopithecine might have been, he would not have been able to oppose a Roman legion effectively unless he could teach a comparable discipline to his fellow lions, gorillas, or australopithecines.

The old battles between spermists and ovists have receded into history. This either-or dispute has been settled with a both-and solution. We now know that both the sperm and the egg contribute, more or less equally, to the genetic constitution of the zygote. Although the old nature-nurture controversy lives on in several guises (for example, biological versus cultural evolution), our geneticists, at least, now recognize that both genetic and environmental factors are required for life. But the debate about the nature of our "innate" urges continues with unabated virulence. Our ancestors were either-or animals who could see in a flash when it was either us or them. Like our ancestors, we are quick to take sides in either-or squabbles, and when the fur begins to fly it obscures any both-and solutions.

Ashley Montagu has recently mustered a platoon of "innate peace" authors in an attack on the implications of Lorenz and Ardrey that we are innately aggressive. The book edited by Montagu, *Man and Aggression*, was reviewed by S. L. Washburn* — who said that Montagu's interpretation of primate behavior is as inaccurate and biased as Ardrey's. According to Washburn, the gentle, cooperative nonhuman primate is as much a product of the imagination as the killer ape. Montagu's contingent asserts repeatedly in this book that nonhuman primates do not kill other members of their own species, but Washburn exposes these statements as false. Macaque monkeys kill macaques, and langur monkeys kill langurs. Ritchie Calder† says it is now generally recognized that *healthy* wild primate societies do not fight *seriously* either within or between bands, and that the *innate* relationships among primates are more *civilized* than the Geneva Convention. The italicized words can be used to mold evidence into almost any desired interpretation. Killer macaques and langurs can be called "unhealthy," the death of their subhuman victims may not be "serious," and the behavior that led to the killing may

* New York *Times*, October 5, 1968.
† *Philosophical Transactions of the Royal Society of London*, Series B, 251 (1966), pp. 451–455.

not have been "innate." The word *civilized*, however, remains a problem. If human warfare began as a sinful response to *civilized* vices, and if *innate* behavior is unlearned, automatic, and uncontaminated by civilization, can we hold up the monkeys and apes as paragons of civilization? Attempts to prove that our innate urges are *either* purely peaceful *or* purely aggressive can draw us into whirlpools of confusion.

Behavior as complex as human warfare is *both* innate *and* intelligent. It requires social organization, which in turn requires *learning*. It is always an intergroup phenomenon. The warriors *learn* to distinguish friend from foe. They often wear uniforms in order to help them do this, and some primitive tribes scarify their faces or wear bones in their noses. Human warfare is not possible in the absence of human sets of genes, and the ability to carry it out is therefore inherited — in the genetic sense. Attempts to distinguish between "innate" and "intelligent" human behavior on an either-or basis are about as meaningful as attempts to decide whether an automobile runs because of its wheels *or* because of its engine. Civilized men also need training before they can achieve the fighting pitch, the discipline, and the confidence in their comrades, required in a large modern army. Men may feel instinctive urges to fight, just as a bitch may feel an urge to growl, but both men and dogs can be trained to suppress such urges. Men can hold their fire until they see the whites of their enemies' eyes. Soldiers who have just killed enemies whose courage they greatly admired can be submissive in the presence of officers they detest. Men who are called primitive, timid, and mild are often as courageous, individually, as anyone else.

There is at least one body of evidence from the Pleistocene itself that is not easily explained in terms of peace without resorting to violence. Neanderthal man disappeared abruptly from western Europe when Cro-Magnon man first appeared in the area. According to William Howells, this "is one of the clearest events of human history." * We are dealing here with prehistoric man in the full sense, for the event took place between 45,000 and 30,000 years ago, twenty to thirty thousand years before the discovery of agriculture. F. Clark Howell refers to this great evolutionary event as follows:

In addition to stopping abruptly, the classic Neanderthaler is replaced with equal abruptness by people like ourselves. There is no blending, no gradual shading from one type to the other. It is as if modern men came storming in and dispossessed the Neanderthalers — perhaps even killed them.†

Howell passes quickly on at this point to a discussion of the problem of whether or not the two kinds of men belonged to the same species, but if killing was in fact involved, then warfare was under way on a subcontinental scale during the Pleistocene.

* Howells is using the term *history* in the broad sense that includes prehistory.
† Carleton Coon suspects that there may have been more blending between the two types of men than this statement implies.

Neanderthal man was replaced by men like ourselves, and men like ourselves have been killing one another for at least five thousand years. If the behavior as well as the anatomy of Cro-Magnon man was like ours, then we should try to remember both the Alamo and Pearl Harbor as we speculate on peaceful coexistence in the Pleistocene. The onus of proof must surely fall to those who assume that peace prevailed. In order to prove that battles to the death did *not* occur (and it is *this* that we must "prove"), a body of evidence must be produced that *outweighs* the massive historical evidence of human warfare.

William Howells deals with the problem in these words:

And the conservative position is to view the Upper Paleolithic people as Whites, coming in and dispossessing Neanderthals. Of course, this eviction did not happen overnight. Nor do we know how it happened, and whether we may imagine the two kinds of men doing battle to the death. *But almost certainly they did not.* The newcomers might, in fact, have extinguished the Mousterians simply by more successful hunting, getting the game first. But the two might have met, even peaceably, and with some slight interbreeding; however, in Europe at least, the probabilities are against more than this. For they would have been naturally hostile competitors, having different ideas and speaking different languages, like the Navahos and the Pueblos, or the Iroquois and Algonquin — and we should not suppose that such tribes were any more openminded about foreign competition than we are. Furthermore, there were probably important spots, avenues of game, or critical passes, such as the meeting of the valleys at Les Eyzies. There must have been real rivalry for command of these, just as bands of Australian aborigines view infringement of their rights to water holes as a fighting matter. [my italics]

There is a flaw in this line of reasoning that may be charitably overlooked, or even defended, by believers in prehistoric peace. Howells sees the two kinds of men as naturally hostile competitors; he does not see them as any more open-minded about foreign competition than we are; he sees great rivalry for the command of important spots; but in spite of all this he is almost certain that battles to the death did *not* take place. He bases this opinion on the argument that the newcomers "might have extinguished the Mousterians simply by more successful hunting." But such a process is easier to suggest than to explain convincingly. Did the Mousterians (Neanderthalers) simply sit down and starve? Game must have persisted in the general area, and they had been killing such game for thousands of years. South African Bushmen killed not only the indigenous game but also the livestock of the invading Dutch (along with a few of the Dutch themselves). Judging from the size of some of the game the Neanderthalers killed, they were neither cowardly nor helpless. Although the American Indians got the "buffalo" first, the invading Europeans took such a full bag later on that the buffalo very nearly followed Neanderthal man into extinction. But Sitting Bull was not the only Indian who objected violently, and General

Custer was not the only invader who died as a result. Neanderthal men may have been less hopelessly outclassed technologically than were the American Indians, and we have no good reason to assume that they were any less courageous.

Unwanted explanations are often discarded on the grounds that they haven't been proved. E. S. Higgs,* for example, refers to the sharp and sudden change from Mousterian to Upper Paleolithic "tool industries" in western Greece, then hastens to add that prehistoric invasions and movements of peoples are difficult to prove. He does not make his point entirely clear, but he is probably not suggesting that all the Neanderthal men in western Europe suddenly "mutated" into Cro-Magnon men. Directly after his reference to this particular case, Higgs hastens to divert attention from it by emphasizing the difficulties involved in proving invasions in certain *other* cases where the archaeological evidence strongly suggests them. But in the case of Neanderthal and Cro-Magnon men, Howell and Howells recognize a sudden *anatomical* change.† Any such anatomical change must

* *The Listener* (London: B.B.C., 1967), Vol. 77, pp. 425–427.

† Howell and Howells assume there *was* a sudden anatomical change, and if Higgs agrees with them he cannot explain such a change in terms of purely "cultural" diffusion. Carleton Coon, however, does not concur with Howell and Howells on the absence of evidence for genetic blending between Neanderthal and Cro-Magnon men in western Europe. He suspects that there may be as many Neanderthal genes in modern Europeans as there are Ainu genes in Japanese, and claims that the only *real* change from Mousterian to Aurignacian and Perigordian was the invention of the punched blade. He has published evidence (*The Seven Caves*, 1957) suggesting that this technique was invented in Syria, and then spread rapidly into Europe — along with Cro-Magnon genes.

have been due to an invasion, or else to a more or less simultaneous production of Cro-Magnon babies by Neanderthal mothers over the whole of western Europe. It is relatively easy to "explain" a cultural change purely in terms of peacefully flowing ideas and implements.* If no striking anatomical changes are involved, it is possible to accept this preferred interpretation on the grounds that the more disturbing one has not been proved. We can point to Japan as "proof" that ideas and implements can "flow" without a corresponding flow of genes (in people).† But the Japanese did not begin to resemble Europeans physically as they learned western industrial techniques.

F. Clark Howell is less "certain" as to how Neanderthal man disappeared. He says an extermination may or may not have taken place, leaving the question wide open while he himself sits squarely on the fence. This is a bit more scientific, but it is rather like saying that "heads" may or may not appear fifty times in a row on an unbiased coin. The layman deserves a better assessment than this from his authorities.

We cannot be *certain* that Neanderthal and Cro-Magnon men fought battles to the death, but science deals with *probabilities*. It is not necessary to "prove" every point in science with utter and absolute rigor. Scientists do not find it difficult to accept the possibility

* Although it is often as difficult to disprove an invasion as it is to prove it, archaeologists usually prefer the more peaceful alternative.

† When we are supporting our favorite beliefs we allow ourselves to assume that living men resemble fossil men; it is mainly in their peacefulness that fossil men are held to have differed so strikingly from us.

that the wings of birds, and the nervous systems that make the flight of birds possible, were inherited from remote ancestors. Even without fossil evidence of any kind it would be generally accepted as entirely reasonable to conclude that prehistoric birds and bats flew, merely from the outstanding aerial performances that have been observed in their descendants. In the same *general* way we can draw indirect inferences about prehistoric social behavior from the remarkable military performances of historical men.* The significance of this possibility has been obscured — not by contrary evidence, but by traditional habits of thought (or by "myths," as Ashley Montagu might put it).

The key to success in war, or in almost any other distinctively human pursuit, is cooperation. All primates are "peaceful" when they cooperate, and they cooperate in order to survive. Studies of primitive peacefulness can be carried out from this point of view.

In Lucy Mair's survey of native African governments, the most primitive culture studied was that of the Nuer cattle herders, who leave their villages during the dry season to follow the receding waters. During this crucial period around shrinking watering places, the separate groups must be able to live in relative peace. The nearest approach to a lawmaker in Nuer communities is called a "leopard-skin chief." He mediates disputes and attempts to settle feuds, but has no right to *command* obedience.

* Without, of course, expecting prehistoric use of napalm or nuclear weapons.

He tries to settle, not to promote, disputes that threaten to become violent.

The task of the leopard-skin chief cannot always be easy. An ideal standard of conduct in Nuer society is for a man to retaliate quickly against an offense. If he is afraid to fight for his rights, he must assume they will not be respected. A man of honor is expected to fight on very slight provocation, and honor has probably always been defined in terms of a capacity to quarrel, perhaps along the lines of Hamlet's concept of greatness:

> Rightly to be great
> Is not to stir without great argument,
> But greatly to find quarrel in a straw
> When honor's at the stake.

Trial by single combat may have begun in the mists of prehistory, and it has of course persisted well into historical times. It was widely assumed that the gods intervene on the side of the right, and since early gods were usually gods of war, the most warlike morals (and muscles) were favored. This primeval life-for-a-life commandment is a source of feuds, and the trouble with feuds is their tendency to continue, or even to escalate. They have been a human problem from the early Egyptians to the Macdonalds and Campbells, and mechanisms for controlling them now range from the Nuer leopard-skin chief to the United Nations. These mechanisms, though not always successful, have evolved along with blood vengeance because feuds undermine capacities for tribal defense. Nuer families were often urged by friends to accept a payment less drastic than full blood vengeance, perhaps in the form of cattle — but the family or village that sold its lives for cattle was clearly less "honorable" than one that demanded two lives for every one of its own. Those who could exact full vengeance were in a better position to quarrel over straws.

Every man was his own policeman in a Nuer village, but he could often count on support from his family or faction. The deterrent effects of clubs and spears in other people's hands restrained both individuals and factions from becoming too ruggedly individualistic. Similar rules applied to *groups* of villages, but here the ties of friendship afforded less protection. Different villages are separated by space, and though family connections may exist between them, there is less daily face-to-face association and people of other villages tend to become strangers. When young Nuer men visited other villages, Mair says, they went in groups, with spears ever ready, and so razor sharp that an accidental contact could draw blood. Killing in fights between different tribes did not fall under the same vengeance law; this was *war*. Mair defines a political community as "that group within which compensation is payable for homicide." This crucial boundary between friend and foe, "them" and "us," "goods" and "bads" may expand, contract, and shift with disarming and unpredictable swiftness. Its breadth and scope at a given time and place can be taken as a measure of civilization.

Perhaps the most significant feature of the Nuer "natural government" is that excessive violence was held in check by a constant threat of violence — from the parent-child to the intertribal level. Modern nations are held together in the same way. Civilized men obey their laws because they know that large and well-organized police forces support the verdicts of juries and the sentences of judges.

There is a fashionable cult in our Great Societies of today that condemns our megalopolises and our computerized affluence, and blames the mighty juggernaut of our social organization for all our ills. Writers mourn for the good old days, and wistfully wish we could turn back the clock and regain the "simple" life of small agricultural groups. Just as we can remember our childhood with an indulgent nostalgia that excludes the tantrums and the growing pains, so we can dream of the "good old days" of small-group life without recalling the bloody and brutal fighting between the groups. This susceptibility to naïve and romantic nostalgia is not peculiar to modern man. The ancient Greeks found release from the brutal realities of their petty little wars by dreaming of a lost Golden Age. The early Hebrews dreamed of a lost Garden of Eden while they struggled with the savage realities of the second millennium B.C. The doctrine of prehistoric peace is not new, nor is it hard to understand. We all need release, if only in our dreams, from the relentless social pressures we apply to one another.

Such dreams, however, are childish — they are more

becoming in Elliot Smith's primitive "children" than in those of us who live in the luxury of the ivory towers that our juggernaut of civilization has built for us. It is, in fact, ironic to note that the primitive "children" who still live in the tattered remains of the "good old days" seem to value our civilization more highly than our dreamers do. Eskimos buy television sets before a transmitter can send programs to them. Eskimo women value their portable sewing machines as highly as their men value their outboard motors. "Underdeveloped" nations are straining to emulate the more prosperous nations. Native arts and skills are abandoned in favor of the products of modern factories. Even the "victims" of high civilization carry with them all the comforts of modern technology they can haul as they pour by the thousands into national parks in search of the "simple life" of bygone days.

There are surely features of the prehistoric life that we still need. The finest nerve endings in our brains and the most exquisite chemical balances between our hormones have evolved for millions of years in a setting of trees and water, blue skies and starry nights, and breezes that rustle leaves and send undulating waves of motion rolling over vast seas of grass. We still need such things, and we often yearn for them amid the jangle of our asphalt jungles. But we do not need the chunk of the tomahawk into the child's skull, or the charred heaps of burned bodies, or the swollen bellies of starving babies that stimulate men to kill in retaliation. We do not need these things, and we do not yearn for them, even though our ancestors have lived in intimate contact with them for millions of years. We will not rid ourselves of these things by yearning nostalgically for an illusion of a lost golden age.

If mankind can outgrow his adolescence and survive, the way is forward, not backward. The starving millions of the world will not be fed by self-centered little city-states like those of ancient Greece, and savage little wars will not be prevented by millions of savagely independent little social groups. Only an even mightier juggernaut of even more complex and all-pervading social organization can establish and maintain global law and order.

VIII

GOLDEN RULES AND PROMISED LANDS

COOPERATION-FOR-CONFLICT has probably always been the key to human survival. Follow the golden rule of cooperation with your neighbors and you may be able to help each other to conquer your Promised Land. This theme is very clear in the early books of the Old Testament. The early Hebrews were commanded sternly to keep away from other people's gods. There was only one Chosen People, and if these could hold together as their numbers increased — rather than "bud off" an endless succession of interhostile little bands — they might become strong enough to conquer Canaan.

The early Hebrews were probably very much like other small Semitic "tribes" of their time. We know there was a great host of interhostile little groups in the Near East during the second millennium B.C., and in its youth the tribe of Abraham, Isaac, and Jacob was a very humble component of this maelstrom. About seven hundred years after the battle between Lagash and Umma the embryonic little band left the city of Ur, about seventy miles south of Lagash. It was probably swept outward by pressures in the heart of the Mesopotamian "hot center." Abram (later Abraham) liked the look of the Jordan valley, but it was not empty. It was seething with a bewildering variety of small warlike groups. These little groups were not all equal, either genetically or in military power. Some were mainly Semitic, others mainly Indo-European, and most were probably genetic conglomerations of the two. Some were bigger than others, and had bigger armies. They included the subjects of the Tidal King of nations, and kings of Shinar, Ellasar, Elam, Sodom, Gomorrah, Admah, Zeboum, and Bela — as well as tribes called Rephaims, Zuzims, Emims, Horites, Amelekites, Amorites, Canaanites, Hittites, Hivites, Perizzites, Girgashites, Jebusites, Kenites, Kenizzites, Kadmonites, Moabites, and others. The size of the social units involved in these savage little struggles can be estimated, roughly, by comparing this list with the size of the small southeastern corner of the Mediterranean coast that contained them all. The state of "international" affairs in this small area must have been rather like that in Sumer seven centuries earlier, or that in New York State in the year 1600.

Abram's little band was too weak to conquer and hold a fertile niche on this unruly frontier, and when famine strikes, its first victims are those who are living on poor land. Famine struck the Jordan valley while Abram was there, and he led his hungry little group to Egypt, which, being socially organized on a relatively large scale, had little to fear from small bands of immigrants. If all the Hebrews followed the example of their leader, introducing their wives as their sisters, the powerful Egyptian aristocrats may have seen recreational possibilities in throwing wide their gates. After his expulsion from Egypt, Abram succeeded in pitching his tents in a small corner of the Promised Land about twenty miles west of the Dead Sea. He wisely refrained from participation in the complex network of petty, but painful, wars that were raging between more powerful kings and tribes. These other groups seem to have been more interested in each other's possessions than in Abram's, and the little band was left in relative peace. Abram did not escape involvement altogether, for his nephew Lot was carried off as a captive. He was able to raise a raiding force of 318 men, which was adequate for the rescue of Lot — but not for the conquest of all Canaan.

Abram's ultimate aim was still the overthrow of all Canaanite "governments," but he was far too intelligent to attempt this while his own tribe was so small. The important objectives of the moment were (1) tribal unity and (2) reproduction.

During his sojourn in Egypt he had seen the power and wealth conferred by large-scale cooperation, so he discouraged his people from making little idols of their own as their numbers increased. Human groups had been drifting apart into disunited social units for about two million years, and it was not easy to break the habit. Disciplinary action against splinter-group formation was necessary, and it was often severe.

During these early days, attacks on foreign groups were frowned upon — because they were likely to bring stronger reprisals than the tribe could repel. When Simeon and Levi reacted to the peaceful genetic exchange between Shechem and Dinah by massacring all males in the Hivite city, Jacob was annoyed — not through any trace of sympathy for the massacred Hivites, but because the attack would make him "stink among the inhabitants of the land" while his own tribe was still "few in number." It was often a matter of life and death to be large in number in those days; if you were not, it was wise to diffuse outward from the general area soon after having offended the senses of more powerful groups. Jacob was advised to move his tribe to Bethel directly after the indiscretions of Shechem, Dinah, Simeon, and Levi. They would have to pass through hostile territory while they were still "stinking" from the massacre. Such movements and social pressures were probably fairly frequent in hot centers. Jacob told his people to purify themselves. They did this by delivering all their "strange gods" to Jacob, who hid them under a tree. Purged of their disunity, they marched forth under a single banner and struck terror upon the cities round about them. They were not attacked or pursued as they fled to Bethel. Fear of hostile foreigners has probably always been the most effective promoter of social unity among related bands of people. We must not forget, however, that Jacob's people were in flight; they had not struck terror enough on the cities around them to make it safe for them to stay near the scene of Simeon and Levi's rampage.

The Old Testament tells of one famine after another in the early days. Some of these may have been general, affecting the strong along with the weak. Others were clearly local, affecting the have-nots more severely than the haves. When Joseph was well installed in his high post in Egypt, the tribe that had sold him into slavery began to feel the effects of a local famine. Rich Egyptians, and Joseph, were suffering less severely from this famine — and Joseph magnanimously arranged for his brothers' people to be settled on fertile land behind the protective shield of the Egyptian army. Under these far more favorable circumstances the early Hebrews spent less time defending themselves and looking for food. They were able to concentrate on the far more important and congenial business of increasing their numbers. They were very successful at this while they were in Egypt, and when they left they are said to have numbered 603,550 males "over twenty who were able to go to war."

This enormous force was not well organized, or it would have made an about-turn and conquered Egypt herself. Smaller armies had conquered all of Mesopotamia, or all of Anatolia. Napoleon invaded Russia with only about 650,000 men. Moses was well aware of the importance of discipline and cooperation within large armies, and he had learned a great deal from his employment in Egypt. But holding an army of over six hundred thousand men together is not easy at any time, and it must have been very difficult indeed when rations had to be found in the hot sands of the Sinai peninsula during the second millennium B.C. Starvation must have been staring the multitudinous Israelites squarely in the face during the Wilderness period, and their single alternative must have been to move onward. The time had finally arrived for the conquest of Canaan — or else.

Land has always been essential to human life. Men have often fought and died for it. In the late second millennium B.C. the haves who were living on milk and honey in the Promised Land were descended from a long line of ancestors who had fought to the death over land. A multitude of Canaanites were bickering over good land in the Jordan valley, and a multitude of Israelites were bickering over poor land on the Sinai peninsula. The victors in the impending holocaust would be those who could most effectively suppress internal dissension within their own ranks. Moses proceeded to do this with great energy. When certain Israelite tribes grumbled at the hardships of the Wilderness, "fiery snakes" were sent to bite them. The descendants of the impetuous Levi lost three thousand men when brothers killed brothers and companions, neighbors. On other occasions the very earth opened to swallow recalcitrant Israelites. When 250 deviants were "consumed," and Moses and Aaron were suspected of having "consumed" them, a plague was brought down on their accusers that carried off 14,700. Even after the *ability* to learn large-scale social cooperation had evolved, the actual learning was often painfully difficult.

The simultaneous importance of warfare and social cooperation is overwhelmingly obvious in the early books of the Old Testament. It was important to rally in large numbers under one god, since those who failed to do so were being slaughtered wholesale. In the nutcracker area between Egypt and Mesopotamia, warfare was a *religion*, in a very literal sense. The religion of Moses and Joshua was not an unusual one. The multitude of little gods differed mainly in the people they had chosen as their own. All of them were savage, all were parching with thirst for the blood of those who refused to worship them. E. E. Kellett compares the Hebrew Yahweh with the gods of other tribes in these words:

When the king of Arad, the Canaanite, came and fought against Israel, and took some of them captive, Israel vowed a vow unto Yahweh and said, "If thou wilt deliver this people into my hand, I will put their cities to the *herem*" — that is, "I will sacrifice them utterly, and without exception." And Yahweh hearkened to the voice of Israel, and delivered the Canaanites into their hand, and they put the cities to the *herem*; and the name of the place was called Hormah, or "Utter Destruction." The same was the fate of Amalek, of Jericho, of Ai: and "Joshua did to the king of Makkedah as he had done to the king of Jericho." The blackened walls of these cities can still be seen, a lasting witness of the terrible savagery which a savage nation can ascribe to a god they fashion in their own likeness. This is exactly parallel to Shalmaneser's account of the battle of Karkar: "With the might which Asshur the Lord has given me, and with the weapons which Nergal, going before me, has bestowed upon me, I fought with the enemy, and made an end of them. Fourteen thousand of their warriors I caused to be slain with the sword." Or we may compare the inscription of Mesha of Moab — who had, it is true, many wrongs to avenge — "And

Chemosh said to me, Go up against the city and take it. And I fought against the city of Kiriathaim and took it, and I strangled every man that was therein as a sacrifice to Chemosh, god of Moab." There is but little difference, save in name, between Yahweh and Asshur or Chemosh, or between the Chosen People, at this stage of their history, and those which were not chosen.

The ferocity of the early Hebrew religion also stands out boldly in these words from the Book of Joshua, chapter 11:

For it was of the Lord to harden their hearts, that they should come against Israel in battle, that he might destroy them utterly, and that they might have no favour, but that he might destroy them, as the Lord commanded Moses.

The destruction of enemies was very clearly a religious matter in those days. When Joshua's armies were united and large in number there was no trace of supplication in his heart. He did not introduce his wives as his sisters when he met powerful Canaanites. He did not even seek their surrender. He wanted them to attack him so he could destroy them, utterly, babies and all. *This* was the religion of the early Hebrews, and it was not peculiar to them. The men who destroyed the cities of Mycenaean Greece had similar motives, and morals. The obscure tribes who fled before them as Sea Peoples were also seeking land, and those who conquered it held themselves together in armies large enough to deal with other armies. The rule of the day can be summarized in one word: *survive*. The key to survival was cooperation-for-conflict. It is not surprising, therefore, to find the Hebrew religion stressing this primeval two-in-one commandment. Human brains can devise an infinitude of religions, but only those who found this key have survived.

According to Kellett there was no morality in the more primitive religions. Most people today would think it immoral to harden people's hearts and then slaughter them, babies and all. But let us pause before we cast stones at the early religions. Joshua's armies worked hard, for some years, to slaughter the Canaanites. Today we can kill more babies than ever lived during Joshua's time, merely by pressing a button. Our religious leaders are divided as to the morality of button-pressing, but very few of them are overturning the money tables. We are rather like Lewis Carroll's walrus, who deeply sympathized, as we prepare to fry the little oysters, every one.

Primitive religions were not *completely* immoral, even in the modern sense. All the successful ones had a commandment, or a complex network of rules and gods, which amounted to: Love thy neighbor. Not many people qualified as neighbors, it is true, but they had to start somewhere, and charity begins at home. It is easier to love the ancient Greeks, or the Iroquois, from the safe distance of several centuries than it is to love the neighbor whose dog persistently anoints our favorite flowers. The family cooperation within small primitive groups of men was, in embryonic form, the ancestor of our confused yearnings for *global* cooperation, or a Brotherhood of Man, today. With all their savage malevolence toward those who lived beyond the pale, primitive religions were probably the medium through which early men struggled toward what we now call morality. These early superstitions were also the embryonic ancestors of modern science, for they all tried, each in its own befuddled way, to explain and interpret the forces of nature. From the depths of their deep primeval desires to *survive*, primitive men mobilized all the capacities for cooperation and sympathy with neighbors that their brains and endocrine systems could muster at the time. They enshrined these little distillations in their religions, and under the banners of these religions they scattered the genes that made their religions possible to the ends of the earth. Today we have brains enough to realize that global cooperation is no mere fuzzy ideal of squeamish intellectuals, but a stark necessity for the survival of our entire species. Most of us can understand this, occasionally, when we snatch a few moments for meditation, and think very hard. Whether we like it or not, we can now do this thanks to the savage cooperation-for-conflict that primitive religions demanded of our ancestors. We are the children of the winners.

There must have been a time when not a single brain on earth was *physically* able to conceive of the earth as a whole, let alone imagine the peaceful cooperation of everyone on it by means of messages traveling at the speed of light. The vast majority of the soldiers who marched onward as to war were not Christians, and most of their brains were quite unable to deal with such prob-

lems as how the words *as to* could have found their way
into the Christian hymn. It is not very likely that australopithecines were physically capable of such mental feats.
Their brains averaged only a third the size of ours, and
there simply wasn't room enough in their skulls for the
required number of nerve connections. The transformation from ape to man was a *gradual* one. No australopithecine mother gave birth to a modern human baby. As
brains increased, gradually, in size and complexity, their
abilities to cope with such abstractions as the advantages
of intergroup cooperation must also have increased, but
very gradually. At any one stage in the process the concepts that were to seem simple and elementary to the
larger brains of future generations must have been confused and only dimly perceived by the brains of the time.
They probably felt "hunches" and "saw" fleeting
glimpses of interrelationships that were later to be
"seen" far more clearly, and in a far broader context, by
larger and more efficient brains. There was always a
Great Unknown that they could almost, but not quite, see
clearly, beckoning to them from the misty frontiers of
their thinking abilities. Every schoolboy knows this feeling well, and carries fears of his Great Unknown with
him into the examination room. His very fears of it, however, spur him on to greater efforts, and sometimes he
leaves with a better understanding of the implications of
the fact that two and two make four.

Joshua's brain probably contained a network of nerve
circuits that would have been adequate for learning
global cooperation had he been taught it from infancy,

and had the people around him behaved in a way that gave him reason to believe it might be possible. But Joshua was reared in the second millennium B.C., and excessive preoccupation with *global* cooperation could well have been fatal then. The stern order of the day was cooperation on a scale that could ensure survival in a very competitive environment. His Israelites were starving in the Wilderness while Canaanites were living on land that was Promised to somebody else. There wasn't room enough for everyone, and if Joshua's host was to have it they must first clear Canaan of Canaanites, once and for all. The religion of the Israelites exhorted them passionately to do this, and do it well. Joshua obeyed the commandments of his religion to the letter, or at least to the very best of his ability. It is said that all who breathed were put to the sword in some thirty-one Canaanite cities, but a few stragglers may have escaped by remaining hidden in the rubble. Joshua can hardly be blamed for missing these. Even Genghis Khan, in much later days, had trouble getting every last one (he is said to have left detachments behind, with orders to wait quietly in the rubble until the cats and chickens and children who had survived the initial holocaust emerged cautiously into the deceptively peaceful stillness). Joshua did as thorough a job of clearing Canaan as we have any right to expect of him. Even a full-scale nuclear war might leave a few survivors. There was a bit of backsliding here and there in Joshua's armies, but much of this was excusable, even in the hungry eyes of Yahweh. The hardworking Hebrew soldiers were allowed to keep a few crumbs of loot for themselves. Yahweh did not always demand *herem* treatment, and permitted a little *harem*-enlargement now and then. This did not, however, leave Canaan seriously cluttered with Canaanites, for the seed of Abraham and Jacob was promptly planted in these concubines, and their offspring were therefore only half Canaanite.

During the second millennium B.C. many tribes failed to achieve the social unity required for the conquest of such an area as Canaan. This was often due to faulty training; not all tribes worshiped gods who saw the importance of cooperation for conflict as clearly as Yahweh did. Many good combinations of genes were destroyed in the general melee. But nature is prodigal. Every step in the process of human development involves a great wastage of promising genes. Purely by chance, millions of sperms fail to fertilize eggs. Unborn babies die when the mothers who carry them suffer misfortunes. After birth, sheer bad luck continues to eliminate otherwise hopeful sets of genes. But those that actually survive to reproduce themselves must escape not only the clutches of bad luck, but also those of humans who seek to destroy them — and this requires brains as well as luck.

Did human learning ability increase during the second millennium B.C.? On the average, were the people who saw the dawn of the Christian Era better able to understand the importance of large-scale social cooperation than those who saw the dawn of the second millennium? If they were, this might help to explain the expansion of human sympathies that can be followed through the latter books of the Old Testament and into the New Testament. If we keep these possibilities in mind we may be able to study the savage emotions of the Old Testament with greater tolerance and understanding. We do not expect chimpanzees or baboons to learn the complexities of our moral codes, and we can hardly blame primitive men for not having done so if their *physical* brains were simply not up to the task.

It might be possible to understand the savagery of early religions more clearly through studies of people who are now living in a primitive "state of nature." Such people are not easy to find now that the "shadow" of our civilization is falling on almost every part of the earth. A few linger on, however, in out-of-the-way places like New Guinea.

The Kurelu tribe of New Guinea was at war with a related tribe called the Wattaia, which lived so near to them that they could shout insults at one another. The actual battles observed by the Harvard-Peabody expedition were often "more noisy than sanguinary," but the two tribes were constant threats to one another, and they frequently sent out raiding parties whose sole purpose was to stalk, and kill, *any* individual. The spearing of an old woman or a little girl was "ample reason for a victory singing." The reason for this savagery was fairly obvious. The greatest threat to the survival of every individual in one group was the other *group*, as a whole. *Any* reduction in the total strength of this other group was glad tidings. During the six months of observation, a series of killings, revenges, reprisals, and counterrevenges took place, and at every moment every individual knew that death might be waiting around the next bend in the path, or at night during sleep. Under these conditions, the emergence of a religion centered on the destruction of enemy lives seems fairly easy to understand. These human enemies were a very real, flesh-and-blood personification of evil in the eyes of people whose deepest instincts were crying out for survival — not only for their own personal survival, but also for that of their own warriors, who stood between them and sudden death under enemy spears.

Matthiessen says that the kains, or war leaders, feared an outbreak of old feuds within the uneasy Kurelu alliance, for it was never certain when such a feud might erupt, and any such dissension in the Kurelu ranks would not only take the form of a merciless civil war, it would weaken the alliance and expose everyone to the mercies of the Wattaia. Moses struggled against similar difficulties in the Wilderness. According to Matthiessen, such a sudden feud would mean that a child protected fiercely as a member of one's own people would become an enemy overnight, "to be killed on sight, without ever being old enough to know the difference."

Men have always feared the unknown, and with very good reason. Rivers have overflowed their banks unexpectedly, drowning many people who were caught unawares. If we could only discover why rivers overflowed, and when they were about to do so, we might be able to get out of their way before they blocked our avenues of escape. Large predators try to keep their presence unknown until it is too late for their intended victims to escape. Surprise attacks can be more effective, at times, than ostentatious advances with much fanfare. They can be very effective at night, when a stealthy approach can be carried out in dark shadows that keep the presence of the raiders *unknown* to their victims. There are many, many ways in which the unknown can be deadly, and men have always had good reason to fear it. When human brains became complex enough to handle the abstractions of a symbolic language, they were also able to invent abstract — or supernatural — explanations of very natural phenomena. The most intense fears probably stimulated the most desperately imaginative mental explorations. Man's most deadly enemy has probably always been man, and it is therefore likely that the most fearful supernatural demons his mind has invented have been inspired by his fear of other men. This possible relationship between human violence and terrifying superstitions seems to be reasonably clear in the following observations of Idriess, who says that one of the first lessons a baby must learn in a band of Australian aborigines is to be quiet at night. During the daytime he is allowed to howl as he wishes, but at night he is hushed if he should merely whimper. This is not due to a fear of snakes or kangaroos. It stems from a fear of hostile men and disembodied spirits:

For an enemy raid may be feared, or the hunters may have detected hurried tracks, crossing their land, or uneasy consciences may fear some prowling vengeance party — a constant, bloodthirsty part of tribal life. Whether or no, there are always the spirit presences of the dark nights to worry the camp, particularly on stormy nights of moaning winds and lightning. Each tribe whispers of certain vicious spirits which are particularly feared, and if these are believed to be prowling round a camp, a tribe can work itself up into a state of hysterical terror.

We must try to avoid the primitive error of leaping prematurely to the conclusion that we understand relationships when we have merely conjured up a picture in our imaginations. Perhaps the relationship between vicious spirits and vengeance parties suggested in the above quotation falls into this category. But on the other hand, perhaps it doesn't. Perhaps the possibility of such a relationship warrants a cautious but careful examination. Just as there seems to be a relationship between gods of war and survival, vendetta killing and fear of reprisal may have something to do with disembodied spirits and uneasy conscience.

Another very early lesson taught to babies in aboriginal Australia was that the tribe was the most important thing on earth. Idriess suggests that this basic law may have "ensured the survival of man throughout the ages." Man has always been his own worst enemy, but he has also been his own best friend. He has always run to "us" for protection against "them."

It has always been easy to "explain" the movements of a bubbling stream, for example, by saying they are due to a "spirit of the stream." Living things seem to have something inside them that makes them move, and this spirit seems to depart when we kill them. It is all too easy to leap from this to the conclusion that all motion must be due to spirits. Many primitive men must have walked away from a stream convinced that they have explained and understood its motion by conjuring up a stream spirit in their own minds. Some of them have had faith enough in this conclusion to leave a little something at the edge of the stream which they thought might tickle the palate of the spirit. Human thoughts and ideas are often "explained" in a similar way, even today.

People who prefer their own ideas to the crudity of physical violence often explain the prehistoric evidence of pots, et cetera, almost entirely in terms of bodiless ideas. Civilization is often assessed in terms of art rather than social cooperation. The ancient Greeks are often held up as paragons of civilization, despite their failure to establish law and order above the level of the small city-state.

Vaillant described the early history of Mexico as a peaceful one, "without external indications of war or revolution." Little idols, et cetera, were traded — without a simultaneous exchange of blows — or carried from village to village by pilgrims. He saw primitive societies as groups of artists: "The history of art is also the history of artists who, in a primitive community, are not a specialized class but the people themselves."

When these primitive artists met, he says, there was often a "ferment of technical and religious experiment," apparently unaccompanied by violence. He even made this statement: "Contact with a foreign source of inspiration brought in a new manner of presentation which may have withered interest in the older technique. Such rhythms appear over and over again in art history."

Primitive art was probably intimately related to primitive religion, and the Islamic holy wars, the Crusades, the Spanish Inquisition, the attitude of early Hebrews to foreign gods, and a host of other examples show clearly that humans do not often discard their religions without a struggle. In Latin America, conversion to Christianity was accomplished by the following "new manner of presentation": Atahualpa, the last emperor of the Incas, was sentenced by Pizarro to be burned alive. He was then told that the sentence could be altered to strangulation if he would accept Christianity. The supreme god of the Incas was the supernatural analogue of Atahualpa himself — and so, when Atahualpa accepted the clemency of the Spaniards, transmutation of one god into the other was possible. Atahualpa was solemnly baptized, then immediately garroted. *This* "manner of presentation" withered interest in the Inca god from one end of Peru to the other.

Nearly all early religions practiced human sacrifice in one form or another. Many peoples seem to have arrived at the idea independently. The Aztecs and the early Hebrews, for example, had never heard of one another. They were very well isolated in both time and space. But both peoples offered up human victims to their gods of war. The differences between these two forms of sacrifice are probably as superficial as language differences, but their common sacrifice of human victims — to gods of war — seems to be as fundamental as the similarities in structure and function of Aztec and Hebrew hearts. Elements of human sacrifice seem to have persisted, even in highly civilized modern nations. The second verse of the British national anthem, for example, begins: "O Lord and God arise, scatter her enemies, and make them fall."

The word *fall* can be interpreted in various ways today, but the original implications are still reasonably clear. The differences between the sentiments expressed in this verse and those expressed on the Aztec altars are considerable, but they are differences in degree, not in kind. The association of supernatural power with the destruction of human enemies probably springs from the same deep, primeval source in Aztecs and British alike — and obedience to the commands of war may account for the very existence of living Aztecs and British in the year 1500. When threatened by desperate and ferocious enemies, prehistoric people did not survive by turning the other cheek.

Some leading biologists still think that the evolution of the brain can never be accounted for in biological terms. Thorpe, for example, says that human mental potentialities have run ahead of any conceivable needs or influence of natural selection, and that the aptitudes and facilities of the human brain are far in excess of what "on any even remotely plausible view" could have been needed at any given point in evolution. The implications of this attitude are fairly clear: we are something above and beyond biology and we cannot be accounted for by "ordinary" processes of evolution. Human brain processes have been mystifying human brains in this way for a long time. We might ask, however, whether or not the aptitudes and facilities of the human brain are far in excess of what is needed at *this* particular point in evolution — and, if so, why Thorpe confessed to: "a feeling of outraged fury when I find spokesmen and authorities in the Christian Churches allowing problems of, say, church order, to absorb their energies out of all proportion to their importance — with the result, or so it seems to me, that this gravest of issues [aggression and war] takes a low place or is ignored."

The aptitudes and facilities of our brains are not so very far in excess of what is needed now, and they may not have been far beyond what was needed at any time in the past, if they have always had to contend with the machinations of other brains. In using the aptitudes and facilities of our brains for studying problems of war and aggression, we should not shrink from a consideration of the savage violence in early religions. Some of our scientists have faced up to the implications of violence to the point of inventing hydrogen bombs. Unless we make very good use of our aptitudes and facilities now, our brains may blow themselves out. We have very good reasons for retaining social cooperation as our golden rule, but "total retaliation" is not very likely to lead us to our Promised Land.

IX

BIOLOGY AND CULTURE

HUMAN CULTURE is generally regarded as something above and beyond "biology." Culture is said to differ *in kind* from things biological, as though it functions on a different and higher plane altogether. A notice from the gallery of South Sea Art in the Bishop Museum in Honolulu expressed this viewpoint in these words:

Many of the pieces in this gallery have a timelessness about them. A timelessness which creates the impression that it is not they who are the result of forces set in motion by the hand of man, but that, rather, they themselves are the forces which have given rise to the motivations which impel man to strive toward a balanced relationship with both the beneficent and the hostile elements in his environment.

The supernatural implications are clear in this statement. There is something "timeless" that seems to enter man from a "higher plane," and this timeless something motivates him to produce works of art — or culture. Levels of culture are almost always gauged in terms of art.

No mundane study of human nature that tries to keep its feet on the ground of biological reality can hope to rule out the possibility of such a supernatural source of motivation. Primitive men have always tried to explain nature in supernatural terms, and the more primitive the men, the more supernatural their explanation seems to have been. Perhaps there was a lost golden age when men were in closer communion with this higher plane of motivation. We cannot rule out this possibility, but we can try to understand the "lower plane" of biology more clearly. If we can do this we may be able to shed some of our arrogant contempt for the "lowly" level of biology, and this may help us to understand how the hand of man can produce works of art.

We have but a dim and superficial comprehension of the intricate coordination of parts in even the tiniest midge that we can hold in our hand. When we think of this midge as a lower form of life we do so because we are very ignorant of the incredible beauty of the system of coordination of all its parts. The midge is so small that we can scarcely see the complexity and precision of its organization. Even when we examine it under a microscope we see only its outer surface. The internal design of its digestive and endocrine and nervous systems is still invisible. The wonders of this tiny marvel of miniaturization lie far beyond the reach of our understanding. Every part of it is related to every other part, in ways that we can only dimly perceive. Yet, in our blindness, we assign this little creature to a lowly biological realm of existence and presume to understand supernatural forces peculiar to ourselves.

Every living creature interacts with other living creatures. The universe that surrounds us, living and dead, is a complex hierarchy of interacting systems. Consider a cat stalking a mouse. Intricately organized chemical processes are taking place in every cell of the cat's body. Complex physiological interactions are taking place between all these countless cells. Each organ system of cells is affecting each other organ system precisely enough, but not too much. This system of systems is producing, before our eyes, a gradual, smooth approach of what appears to us to be a unit — the cat — toward the still unsuspecting mouse. The cat's attention is riveted on the mouse. The mouse looks up. The cat freezes instantly. The large yellow eyes do not move; they continue, nevertheless, to receive the light rays which are stimulating the retinal cells, which are sending a barrage of impulses in code to the brain, which in turn is transmitting a barrage of impulses to the endocrine and muscular systems — but all this is hidden from our eyes. Only the tail, hidden behind its body, has failed to contain the fierce energies inside the otherwise motionless cat. The cat is hungry, but she restrains herself. The mouse looks down. The cat's approach continues silently, the body flowing smoothly forward, low down, near the grass. The legs move carefully forward, feeling for solid, silent footing, but the eyes remain fixed on the mouse. The legs and feet seem to act on their own, without distracting the intense concentration of the cat's brain, and yet the brain is directing their every slow and careful motion. The mouse looks up, sees the cat, and freezes. The cat's hind feet move up and down, finding solid footing, the body begins visibly to quiver — something inside it seems to rise to a climax — and it streaks forward. There is a rapid scuffle, a squeak — the cat looks up, ears back, eyes glaring, and a low growl emerges from the throat. This small drama has involved a complexity of interadjusted and exquisitely coordinated systems-on-systems which lies so far above and beyond our present powers of comprehension that our best attempts to explain it are pathetic. No living human can conceive, let alone communicate, more than a glimpse of the precision, intricacy, and superb coordination of all that took place in the cat — let alone the interactions between it and the mouse, which might have escaped.

We do not object to the biological study of cats and mice and midges, but we do not like to relegate man, and least of all culture, to this low level. Theodosius Dobzhansky, in his *Mankind Evolving*, says that a majority of anthropologists, psychologists, sociologists, and not a few biologists "maintain that biological evolution has achieved the genetic basis of culture and run its course; it is now a matter of the past. The genetic basis of culture is uniform everywhere; cultural evolution has long since taken over."

Dobzhansky does not seriously dispute the logic of this distinction between culture and biology. Other biologists, such as Julian Huxley (1958), emphasize what they consider to be a fundamental difference between "cultural" and "biological" evolution. They consider cultural evolution to be a process in its own right, superimposed upon, but nevertheless distinct and different in kind from, biological evolution. This general view has been stated as follows by Huxley:

As organisms are what evolve in the biological phase of evolution, so cultures are what evolve in its psychosocial or human phase. To put the matter baldly, biological species, with their bodies and their physiological functions, confront the environment with organized systems of self-reproducing matter and its products: the human species does so with organized systems of self-reproducing mind and its products, superimposed on the constituent biological organisms.

This places human culture very neatly out of biological reach. The study of human nature is left to people who lack biological training.

This culture-biology schism is unfortunate, for it diverts attention from the many and intimate interactions between these two allegedly distinct phenomena. Most of our cultural activities have biological side effects. The wooden spear, a product of cultural evolution, doubtless caused many cultural ideas to dance in human heads, but it also enabled many human heads to be removed — and this is a biological event. Such biological events encouraged the invention of the spear-thrower, another cultural product. This, too, had biological effects, which encouraged the invention of the bow and arrow. Each new cultural invention in one region created a "missile gap" that stimulated cultural activity in other regions. The stimulus, however, was not purely cultural — it was also biological. Carleton Coon (1963, p. 123) sees a biological stimulus at the core of all human culture, and suggests that family, economic, political, and religious institutions all arose in response to instinctive motivations. He does not imply that these institutions are therefore blind or mindless, only that they grow from biological soil. An understanding of the biology of human culture will be achieved more rapidly by this both-and approach than by the either-or doctrine that places culture out of biological reach.

The products of human culture also have biological effects on subhuman animals, as when shotgun pellets and rifle bullets enter the bodies of rabbits and deer, or when industrial chemicals kill insects and songbirds alike. Not only Indians were massacred in early Massachusetts; Roger Tory Peterson says that a bounty of one penny per wolf was authorized there in 1630. Neither Indians nor wolves threaten farmers in Massachusetts today — a biological change has been accomplished by human cultural activity. African wildlife is said to be under siege as a result of human snares, traps, firearms, felled forests, plows, and introduced livestock. These cultural activities are producing cataclysmic results. Modern medicine produces a great variety of biological effects — on the flesh that parts beneath the surgeon's knife, on the genetic constitution of mankind as a whole, and on the actual size of the world's population. H. J. Muller and others have expressed concern at the increase in harmful mutant genes that seems to be taking place as an unplanned by-product of human cultural activities. The United Nations Statistical Yearbook of 1965 estimated world population at more than 3.2 billion. Nuclear explosions are physical events produced by human cultural activity, but their biological effects can be widely disseminated through both space and time. In the presence of these biological realities, is it realistic to consider human evolution as "purely cultural"?

Biologists do not hesitate to consider the nest of a bird as a biological phenomenon, even if it is composed entirely of nonliving matter. If men were birds, however, they would probably consider their nests as cultural phenomena. It would be clear that no other animal could build such a wonderful nest, and we would regard it as something quite above and beyond mere biology. But if men were birds, they would not be men, and they would not be able to arrive at such an irrational conclusion. We take such pride in the fact that we are rational animals that we tend to overlook the fact that we are the most *irrational* of all animals. No other animals could fabricate such an amazing fantasia of fairy tales as those that have flitted from human brain to human brain.

Fairy tales seem to be unrelated to the force of gravity. They cannot be weighed on material scales or dissected with steel scalpels. We cannot feel their texture with our fingers. They appear to be bodiless and quite immaterial products of "pure mind." Yet they can alter the chemical constituents of human bodies, sending adrenalin coursing through very material veins and arteries. They can seal the fate of powerful armies. All individual humans who are capable of speech are able to fabricate fairy tales. Young children are often particularly talented in this respect. Just as birds seem to inherit the ability to build a nest, so humans are able to fabricate irrational ideas. This is far easier than learning mathematics.

Each human social group, therefore, has an endless and infinite source of supply from which to construct its own set of beliefs. Once a given set has been accepted by the group, additional fairy tales will be, and must be, rejected — unless they can be fitted into the prevailing structure. Each group requires something intimate, unique to itself, around which its members can cohere. Irrational beliefs serve this purpose far better than rational ones; they are not only easier to produce, but also less likely to be confused with enemy beliefs. All humans tend to accept without question the irrational beliefs of the group to which they belong. We seem to be born with a propensity to *believe* what we are told. We also seem to be born with a tendency to regard the beliefs of *other* social groups as silly, ridiculous, and quite irrational. Foreign beliefs are often regarded as very dangerous, especially if they should infect our friends. Dearly beloved friends have been boiled in oil, burned at stakes, or brainwashed for their own good — to free them from the satanic influence of foreign beliefs. Irrational fantasies produce a continuous supply of "group uniforms," promoting and maintaining internal cohesion *within* each group, and segregation *between* groups.

These irrational group uniforms have survival value —

provided they place enough emphasis on social solidarity within the group, and serve to segregate it from other groups which might destroy or weaken it. It is not necessary for the brains within the group to understand this, but most human brains can grasp the survival value of the primeval difference between "us" and "them." There is an element of rationality in all biologically effective group beliefs — and this rational element is directly and intimately related to sheer biological survival. The trimmings around this functional, biological core of rationality, however, can be highly irrational. Belief in supernatural demons can often stimulate people to huddle together very closely. Rational explanations often have a less cohesive effect, especially when they are not well understood. Science can provide the weapons of war, but not the will to use them.

Today's babies are probably *able* to learn social cooperation on a world scale, but they will *actually* learn what they are taught. Most of them will learn the narrow tribal loyalties and intergroup hostilities that we, their parents, have learned from our own parents and teachers. Christian babies will learn Christian thoughts. Hindu babies will learn Hindu thoughts. All this learning will take place through biological processes involving biological human brains — and such cultural slogans as "imperialist warmonger," "better dead then red," and "two, four, six, eight, we don' wanna integrate" will not be entirely independent of a biological source.

Much has been written about the possible origins of human rationality, natural and supernatural. Less has been written about the origins of human irrationality, and even less about its possible biological and evolutionary origins. So far as we know, only humans are able to deceive and confuse one another with their imaginations. Squids can deceive other animals by squirting a cloud of inky material into the water, thereby distracting attention from the actual squids themselves; but only man can organize inky material into symbolic patterns in a way that can distract attention from reality itself.

X

COOPERATION-FOR-SURVIVAL

NIETZSCHE, VON BERNHARDI, AND KEITH concluded that war was necessary because it is innate in our natures. Two world wars, and the Nazi gas chambers, have been laid at the feet of these doctrines, and many able thinkers have recoiled from them in horror. Most recent books and symposia on human evolution ignore warfare altogether, implying that peace prevailed everywhere for more than two million years. There is no sound basis for the belief that warfare is now necessary or good, but this does not rule out the possibility that it trebled the size of the human brain. It is not rational to ignore this possibility merely through horror of the Nazi superman doctrine. Actually, Nietzsche played a very minor role in World Wars I and II. Many thousands of African slaves were transported before he was born, and the savage battles of the American Civil War were fought without knowledge of his philosophy. The causes of World Wars I and II lie far deeper than any conscious human philosophies, and superrace doctrines are probably as old as man himself. Goals like *Lebensraum* and *Drang nach*

Osten did not first appear in twentieth-century Europe. Similar aims are expressed with brutal clarity in the Old Testament. Every human group that ever lived has been aware of the importance of *Lebensraum*. It is not Nietzschean philosophy that threatens our survival today — it is ignorance of the forces that made us what we are, and the fear of ourselves that this ignorance engenders.

If we are in fact the spawn of the winners of millions of years of war, we can face the fact without leaping to the conclusion that we are doomed. Human warfare is impossible without cooperation, and if our ancestors survived by learning to cooperate for self-defense in ever larger groups, we may have inherited from them the brains required for learning it on a global scale. We already cooperate on a semiglobal scale, and although our values and loyalties are still dangerously circumscribed they have nevertheless advanced far beyond the intervillage level. We live on the rumbling volcano of millions of years of savage violence, and yet we *live* — because the loyalties of our ancestors expanded from the village to embrace the tribe, and then the nation, and then the power bloc of allied nations. Complacency is dangerous, but so is overemphasis on the many gloomy aspects of the present state of affairs.

One of the gloomiest of modern philosophies contends that we are innately peaceful. This implies that we are caught in the coils of a mass insanity, and that our civilization is the source of this enormous evil. If so, the obvious antidote is a return to a "state of nature." If we are in fact the product of millions of years of peaceful evolution, equipped "by nature" only for peace, then we are surely in a very sad predicament. If our civilization is the source of our insanity, and if we cannot give ourselves the psychiatric treatment required to exorcize or dismantle this evil growth, our future is black indeed. In the throes of our madness, equipped by nature only for peace, we can hardly be expected to deal effectively with the insane spectre of war. If such a sorry state of affairs exists, we must face up to it — but the evidence weighs heavily against this depressing conclusion. If the iron self-discipline of a superb warrior is required to restrain the dogs of war in us, at least five thousand years of history suggest that *Homo sapiens* may be that very warrior.

Ardrey and Montagu and others imply that only blind, "subhuman" urges have evolved *genetically* and *biologically*. But what has *actually* evolved is the human brain itself, and the most distinctive feature of this instrument is its ability to weigh and consider — that is, to learn. The particular language or religion an individual learns is not in itself innate, but the *ability* to learn a language or religion can appear only through the action of a *human* set of genes. All mammals are able to learn from experience. Even dogs and baboons can learn to control powerful inner drives of hunger and thirst and sex. We are far better equipped for learning self-control than are any dogs or baboons. We can restrain aggressive drives through conscious, intelligent effort — and such restraint has soared to its highest pinnacles on bloodstained battlefields. We can also suppress our deepest longings for peace — when we are threatened. It is this very ability to weigh and consider — and to control ourselves — that was evolved in the fierce arena of the Pleistocene. Groups that fought blindly and stupidly at the wrong time were exterminated. Groups that surrendered blindly to an "urge" for peace starved or froze on deserts or mountaintops. *We* are the children of the winners. *Our* ancestors made effective decisions, or we would not have been born. We are not at the mercy of entirely blind and uncontrollable urges — either for peace or for war. But we *are* at the mercy of our own ignorance.

If this theory is sound we have cause for confidence, but none whatsoever for complacency. We are still very primitive despite our impressive social achievements, and we may be unable to maintain the social cohesion that holds us together now in the largest blocs of social unity that have ever existed on earth. Perhaps we have overextended ourselves. Perhaps our social cohesion will disintegrate from within, even if we refrain from a total thermonuclear war. Other empires have disintegrated into dark ages of savage violence, and our own civilization is now about as old as those were when they collapsed. Population pressures have had something to do with social collapse in the past, and they are very powerful now, not only in the Negro ghettos of America, but all over the world. Our present achievements, however, remain impressive — despite the riots, the social injustice, the conventional warfare, and even despite the spine-chilling implications of our nuclear arms race. Despite all this, we are still cooperating on an unprecedented scale. Most people who live in large modern nations have never seen two men in mortal combat. (There is a profound difference between images on a screen and the real thing.) Most of us go to our beds without fear of being speared in our sleep by warriors who live within easy walking distance. Neighboring towns are not constantly ready for war with one another as they were in early Sumer or Greece. Despite the horrors of our wars it is probably true that more people have spent more time living at peace with one another in the twentieth century than in any previous period of similar length.

It may be wise now to consider these things, for it is becoming fashionable to see our civilization as an evil weight crushing our individuality. Up to a point, cynicism can be healthy — but if it should undermine our grip on the value of our civilization, we could receive a very rude and violent shock. If we think a return to a "state of nature" would bring us peace, we are deluding ourselves very dangerously.

All humans have values, and all human values are interrelated, even when — or perhaps especially when — they contradict each other directly. Most humans have values that could be drawn together intelligently in a way that could ensure cooperation on a global scale. Our ancestors have given us the genes required for learning cooperation on this enormous scale, and we have almost succeeded — almost but not quite. We do not yet understand ourselves, and so we have not yet found a formula of laws, or values, that can draw all mankind together into a *single* stable and enduring social system. Are we, then, incapable of global cooperation *without* conflict?

This idea has been explored by the lively imaginations of science fiction writers, who spin exciting fantasies of a world united against an external threat — a planet on collision course with ours, or an imminent invasion by extraterrestrial creatures. Faced with a common danger, the great power blocs stop threatening each other and unite against the global foe. These endearing pictures of a united mankind make some people gaze wistfully at the night skies, hoping vaguely that invading Martians might weld us into a common brotherhood — without destroying or enslaving us. There may be an element of such wishful thinking in the many sightings of flying saucers.

In actual fact, we need not look so far afield. A common threat to our whole species is easy to find. We have built it ourselves. Our hydrogen bombs are as lethal as any extraterrestrial dangers our science fiction writers can devise. We are living in a science fiction world of our own making. Will we be able to cope with an environment so different from that of all our ancestors, while we ourselves remain so very much the same? Can we plan and build our future intelligently while we still cling to so many of our primitive myths? Dare we look back to our past, to our primeval origins, in an attempt to understand the forces that made us what we are? Can we curb our capacity for violence and enlarge our hard-won qualities of restraint, forbearance, and tolerance? Despite all the present evidence to the contrary, we have made impressive progress in this direction. In the past two decades, disputes that would have meant all-out war in the preatomic age have been settled by negotiation. Our politicians and statesmen are aware of the global threat.

We are very adaptable, but can we adapt to new conditions quickly enough? The need for a new philosophy is urgent. Due to our technological brilliance, the age-old formula, cooperation-for-conflict, has become a prescription for extinction, not survival. Can we alter this primeval law to cooperation-for-survival? We have inherited brains that can weigh and consider. We have inherited a very impressive capacity for self-control. But can we weigh and consider and control ourselves wisely and well enough as we stand, here and now? If we cannot, our thermonuclear warheads are waiting. They are cold, utterly dumb, and utterly blind. They are creations of what we call "cultural evolution," but they have no trace of human morality. If we press the button, they will destroy us without the slightest qualm. If we dismantle them, they will feel no trace of pain. The decision will be ours, and it will take place in our brains. The urge for peace and the urge for war will both be present, but our brains will actually throw the switch — one way or the other.

REFERENCES

Albright, William F. *Archaeology of Palestine*. Harmondsworth: Penguin, 1949. Revised editions 1954, 1956, 1960; Gloucester, Mass.: Peter Smith, 1960. (Published as: *Archaeology and the Religions of Israel*. Baltimore: Johns Hopkins, 1953.)

Ardrey, Robert. *African Genesis: A Personal Investigation into the Animal Origins and Nature of Man*. New York: Atheneum, 1961; London: Collins, 1961.

——. *The Territorial Imperative: A Personal Inquiry into the Animal Origins of Property and Nations*. New York: Atheneum, 1966; London: Collins, 1967.

Bibby, Geoffrey. *Four Thousand Years Ago: A Panorama of Life in the Second Millennium* B.C. New York: Knopf, 1961; London: Collins, 1962.

Burn, Andrew R. *The Pelican History of Greece*. Harmondsworth: Penguin, 1966. (Originally published as: *A Traveller's History of Greece*. London: Hodder and Stoughton, 1965.)

Childe, V. Gordon. *What Happened in History*. Harmondsworth: Penguin, 1943; London: Max Parrish, 1960.

Churchill, Winston S. *The Birth of Britain*. Vol. 1. A History of the English Speaking People. London: Cassell, 1956.

Coon, Carleton S. "Growth and Development of Social Groups." *Man and His Future*. Edited by Gordon Wolstenholme. London: Churchill, 1963; Boston: Little, Brown, 1963.

——. *The History of Man from the First Human to Primitive Culture and Beyond*. Second edition revised. New York: Knopf, 1962 (a); London: Jonathan Cape, 1962.

——. *The Origin of Races*. New York: Knopf, 1962 (b); London: Jonathan Cape, 1963.

——, and Edward E. Hunt. *The Living Races of Man*. New York: Knopf, 1965; London: Jonathan Cape, 1966.

Crow, James F. "Ionizing Radiation and Evolution." *Scientific American* Offprint No. 55. San Francisco: W. H. Freeman, 1959.

Daniel, Glyn E. *The Megalith Builders of Western Europe*. New edition. Harmondsworth: Penguin, 1963. (Originally published: London: Hutchinson, 1962.)

Dart, Raymond A. "The Predatory Implemental Technique of *Australopithecus*." *American Journal of Physical Anthropology*, new series (1949), Vol. 7, pp. 1–38.

——. "The Predatory Transition from Ape to Man." *International Anthropological and Linguistic Review* (1953), Vol. 1, pp. 208–218.

Darwin, Charles R. *The Descent of Man and Selection in Relation to*

Sex. London: John Murray, 1871–74; new edition, London: John Murray, 1901.

Desborough, Vincent R. d'A. *The Last Mycenaeans and Their Successors: An Archaeological Survey c. 1200–c. 1000 B.C.* Oxford: Clarendon, 1964.

De Vore, Irven, ed. *Primate Behavior: Field Studies of Monkeys and Apes*. New York: Holt, Rinehart and Winston, 1965.

——, and K. Ronald L. Hall. "Baboon Ecology." *Primate Behavior*. Edited by Irven De Vore. New York: Holt, Rinehart and Winston, 1965.

Dobzhansky, Theodosius G. *Mankind Evolving: The Evolution of the Human Species*. New Haven: Yale University Press, 1962.

Ellis, Havelock. *The Philosophy of Conflict, and Other Essays in Wartime*. Second series. Boston: Houghton Mifflin, 1919; London: Constable, 1919.

Goodall, Jane. "Chimpanzees of the Gombe Stream Reserve." *Primate Behavior*. Edited by Irven De Vore. New York: Holt, Rinehart and Winston, 1965.

Hall, K. Ronald L., and Irven De Vore. "Baboon Social Behavior." *Primate Behavior*. Edited by Irven De Vore. New York: Holt, Rinehart and Winston, 1965.

Harlow, Harry F., and Margaret K. "Affectional Systems," *Behavior of Nonhuman Primates: Modern Research Trends*, Vol. 2. Edited by Allan M. Schrier, Harry F. Harlow and Fred Stollnitz. New York: Academic Press, 1965.

Herodotus. *The Histories*. Newly Translated with an Introduction by Aubrey de Selincourt. Harmondsworth: Penguin, 1954.

Hood, Sinclair. *The Home of the Heroes: The Aegean Before the Greeks*. Library of Early Civilizations. Edited by Stuart Piggott. London: Thames and Hudson, 1967.

Howell, F. Clark, with the editors of *Life*. *Early Man*. New York: Time, Inc., 1965.

Howells, William. *Mankind in the Making: The Story of Human Evolution*. Harmondsworth: Penguin, 1967. (Published originally: New York: Doubleday, 1959; London: Secker and Warburg, 1961.)

Huxley, Julian. "Cultural Process and Evolution." *Behavior and Evolution*. Edited by Anne Roe and George Gaylord Simpson. New Haven: Yale University Press, 1958.

——. "Discussion: Eugenics and Genetics," *Man and His Future*. Edited by Gordon Wolstenholme. London: Churchill, 1963. Boston: Little, Brown, 1963.

Idriess, Ion L. *Our Living Stone Age*. London: Angus and Robertson, 1964.

Jay, Phyllis. "Field Studies," *Behavior of Nonhuman Primates: Modern Research Trends*, Vol. 2. Edited by Allan M. Schrier, Harry F. Harlow and Fred Stollnitz. New York: Academic Press, 1965.

Juvaini, 'Ala-ad-Din-Ata-Malik. *The History of the World-Conqueror.* Translated from the Persian text of Mirza Muhammed Quazvini by John Andrew Boyle. Manchester: Manchester University Press, 1958; Cambridge, Mass.: Harvard University Press, 1958.

Kellett, Ernest E. *A Short History of Religions.* New York: Dodd, 1934; London: Gollancz, 1933; Harmondsworth: Penguin, 1962.

Kraus, Bertram S. *The Basis of Human Evolution.* New York: Harper and Row, 1964.

La Farge, Oliver. "The Enduring Indian." *Scientific American* (1960), Vol. 202, pp. 37–45.

——. *A Pictorial History of the American Indian.* New York: Crown, 1956; London: André Deutsch, 1956.

Lasker, Gabriel W. *The Evolution of Man: A Brief Introduction to Physical Anthropology.* New York: Holt, Rinehart and Winston, 1961.

Leechman, J. Douglas. *Native Tribes of Canada.* Scarborough, Ont.: W. J. Gage Ltd., 1956.

Lissner, Ivar. *The Living Past: The Great Civilizations of Mankind.* Translated from the German by J. Maxwell Brownjohn. London: Jonathan Cape, 1957. (Published originally as: *So habt ihr gelebt.* Olten U. Freiburg/Br.: Walter, 1955.)

Lorenz, Konrad. *On Aggression.* Translated from the German by Marjorie Latzke, with a foreword by Julian Huxley. London: Methuen, 1966; New York: Harcourt, Brace and World, 1967. (Published originally as: *Das sogenannte Böse.* Vienna: Borotha-Schoeler, 1963.)

Mair, Lucy P. *Primitive Government.* Harmondsworth: Penguin, 1962.

Mason, J. Alden. *The Ancient Civilizations of Peru.* Harmondsworth: Penguin, 1957.

Matthiessen, Peter. *Under the Mountain Wall: A Chronicle of Two Seasons in the Stone Age.* New York: Viking, 1962; London: Heinemann, 1963.

McEvedy, Colin. *The Penguin Atlas of Ancient History.* Harmondsworth: Penguin, 1967.

——. *The Penguin Atlas of Medieval History.* Harmondsworth: Penguin, 1961.

Montagu, Ashley. *Man in Process.* Cleveland: World Publishing Co., 1961.

Morris, Desmond. *The Naked Ape: A Zoologist's Study of the Human Animal.* London: Jonathan Cape, 1967; New York: McGraw-Hill, 1968.

Muller, Hermann J. "Radiation and Human Mutation." *Scientific American* Offprint No. 29, San Francisco: W. H. Freeman, 1955.

Mumford, Lewis. *The Myth of the Machine: Technics and Human Development.* New York: Harcourt, Brace and World, 1967.

Mylonas, George E. *Mycenae and the Mycenaean Age.* Princeton, N.J.: Princeton University Press, 1966.

Phillips, Eustace D. *The Royal Hordes: Nomad Peoples of the Steppes.* Library of the Early Civilizations. Edited by Stuart Piggott. London: Thames and Hudson, 1965.

Reed, Stephen W. *The Making of Modern New Guinea, with Special Reference to Culture Contact in the Mandated Territory.* Issued in cooperation with the International Secretariat, Institute of Pacific Relations. (*Memoirs*, Vol. 18, Institute of Pacific Relations, International Research Series). Philadelphia: American Philosophical Society, Institute of Pacific Relations, 1943.

Reynolds, Vernon and Frances. "Chimpanzees of the Budongo Forest." *Primate Behavior.* Edited by Irven De Vore. New York: Holt, Rinehart and Winston, 1965.

Rice, Tamara Talbot. *The Scythians.* Ancient Peoples and Places Series. Vol. 2. Edited by Glyn Daniel. New York: F. A. Praeger, 1958; London: Thames and Hudson, 1958.

Roux, Georges. *Ancient Iraq.* London: Allen and Unwin, 1964; Harmondsworth: Penguin, 1966.

Russell, W. M. S. *The Listener*, vol. 77 (April 13, 1967), pp. 487–488.

Samuel, Alan E. *The Mycenaeans in History.* Englewood Cliffs, N. J.: Prentice-Hall, 1966.

Sanderson, Ivan T. *Living Mammals of the World.* London: Hamish Hamilton, 1955.

Schaller, George B. "The Behavior of the Mountain Gorilla." *Primate Behavior.* Edited by Irven De Vore. New York: Holt, Rinehart and Winston, 1965.

Seidler, Grzegorz Leopold. *The Political Doctrine of the Mongols.* Lublin: Nakladem Uniwersytetu Marii Curie-Sklodowskiej, 1960. (Annales Universitatis Mariae Curie-Sklodowska, Lublin, Polonia, Sectio G, Vol. 6, 7.)

Smith, G. Elliot. *Human History.* New York: W. W. Norton, 1929; London: Jonathan Cape, 1930.

Southwick, Charles H., Mirza Azhar Beg, and M. Rafiq Siddiqi. "Rhesus Monkeys in North India." *Primate Behavior.* Edited by Irven De Vore. New York: Holt, Rinehart and Winston, 1965.

Thorpe, William H. *Science, Man and Morals: Based upon the Freemantle Lectures delivered in Balliol College, Oxford, Trinity Term, 1963.* London: Methuen, 1965.

Vaillant, George C. *The Aztecs of Mexico: Origin, Rise and Fall of the Aztec Nation.* American Museum of Natural History Science Series. Vol. 2. Revised by Suzannah B. Vaillant. New York: Doubleday, 1962; Harmondsworth: Penguin, 1962.

Ventris, Michael G. F., and John Chadwick. *Documents in Mycenaean Greek: Three Hundred Selected Tablets from Knossos, Pylos and Mycenae with Commentary and Vocabulary.* Foreword by Alan J. B. Wace. London: Cambridge University Press, 1956.

Vermeule, Emily T. *Greece in the Bronze Age*. Chicago: Chicago University Press, 1964.

Ward, Russel B. *Australia*. Englewood Cliffs, N.J.: Prentice-Hall, 1965.

Washburn, Sherwood L., and Irven De Vore. Film entitled: *Baboon Behavior*. Berkeley: University of California, 1963.

Washburn, Sherwood L., and F. Clark Howell. "Human Evolution and Culture." *Evolution After Darwin*. Vol. 2. Edited by Sol Tax and C. Callender. The University of Chicago Centennial Discussions. Chicago: University of Chicago Press, 1960.

White, Lancelot Law. *The Next Development in Man*. New York: New American Library, 1950.

Williams, Maslyn. *Stone Age Island: Seven Years in New Guinea*. London: Collins, 1964.

Wolstenholme, Gordon, ed. *Man and His Future*. London: Churchill, 1963; Boston: Little, Brown, 1963.

Wright, Sewall. "Evolution in Mendelian Populations." *Genetics* (1931), Vol. 16, pp. 97–159.

INDEX

Aaron, 222
Abimelech, 114
Abraham (Abram), 78, 114, 217–219, 229
Accidents, 51, 126
Achaeans, 75
Achaea, 80
Adamson, Joy, 40
Admiralty Islands, 128
Adultery, 19, 113
Aegean area, 15, 76, 143, 173
Aequi, 175
Aeolians, 76
Africa, 22, 32, 56, 65, 88, 93, 98, 107–108, 110, 113–114, 141n., 142, 147, 156n., 176, 185–186, 188, 191, 211, 244
Aggression, 155–158, 204, 251
Agility, 51
Agriculture, 81–82, 97, 185–186, 193, 197–198, 206, 214. *See also* Food, importance of
Akkad, 140
Alaska, 176
Albright, William, 141–142
Alexander the Great, 135, 144, 167
Altai Mts., 140, 145, 147
America. *See* North America; South America
Amorites, 140–141, 184, 218
An Yang, 85
Anatolia, 16, 66, 69, 74, 90, 142, 221
Ancestors, 5, 21, 67–68, 90, 124, 156, 163, 215, 252–253

Andaman Islanders, 191
Animals, 3, 5, 136, 201–202. *See also* Humans; Primates; *individual animal entries*
Anthropology, 10, 12, 21, 50, 51, 188, 199, 242
Apes, 10, 12, 21, 25, 30–43, 205
Arabian Sea, 171
Arcadia, 80
Archaeology, 10, 62, 68, 99, 154, 172, 194, 209, 210n.
Arctic, the, 52
Ardrey, Robert, 119, 203–204, 251
Argos, Gulf of, 71
Armenoids, 184
Armies, 108, 152, 175, 178, 205, 221, 224. *See also* Soldiers
Art, 234–235. *See also* Cultural evolution
Aryans, 142–144. *See also* Indo-Europeans (Indo-Aryans)
Asia/Asians, 56, 75, 91, 93, 98, 107, 139, 143–144, 149–150, 186; outward flow of genes from, 89, 144, 147–148, 150, 153–154, 175–176, 180. *See also individual country entries;* Eurasia
Asia Minor, 76, 85
Atahualpa, 235
Athens, 70, 79–80, 85
Atlantic Ocean, 56, 176
Attica, 79–80
Attila, 89, 178, 179
Aurignacians, 209n.

Australia, 52, 98, 107, 141n., 176, 186

Australian aborigines, 25, 53, 108, 112–113, 129, 189–191, 197–198, 208, 232–233

Australoid genes, 184n.

Australopithecines, 203; social organization, 21–22, 46; characteristics, 45–46; suspected of killing own species, 46–47; internecine violence, 46, 48; group integration, 47, 53; intergroup violence and war, 47–48, 51, 54–55, 57, 61; restraints, 47; women and children, 48; predation pressure on, 48–49; likely habitations, 51–53; group size, 52; learning abilities, 52; linguistic differences, 53; segregation, 53; competition increase, 53–54; population increase, 54–56; prevalence of better brains, social organizations, armies, 56, 135; assumed polygamous, 115; argument against, as early man, 119–120; example of genetic drift among, 122–123, 125–126; emotions, 136; brains, 227

Avars, 150

Aztecs, 14, 93–95, 102, 177, 235–236

Baboons, 12, 27–28, 32, 51, 230; organization, 4, 47; communication, 5; social cooperation, 10–11, 81; group movement, 11, 22, 29; emergence from Pleistocene, 11; predation on, 22, 183; social rank, 23, 25–26; sex drive, 11, 23–25; stalemate with lions, 22, 49; sublimation of drives, 23–25, 27, 251; fighting ability, 26; subservience, 26, 28; behavior determined by group action, 27–29, 34–35, 37, 109; conflicts among, 31, 46; vs. man, 50; inbreeding, 122–123

Babylonia, 79, 140

Balkans, the, 66, 76

Balkh, 165–166, 168

Bamiyan, 164–165

Barbarians, 74–75

Beavers, 89

Beliefs. See Faith; Humans: rational and irrational beliefs of

Bering Strait, 56, 90–92, 137

Bernhardi, Friedrich von, 249

Bethel, 220

Bibby, Geoffrey, 171–172, 184, 184n., 185–187

Bible, 114, 142, 217, 221, 229–230

Biological evolution, 20, 88–90, 94, 101–102, 203, 236–237, 239–248

Biology, 10, 10n., 104, 126–127. See also Biological evolution

Birds, 201, 211, 245–246

Black Sea, 69, 83, 161, 178

Boeotia, 80

Böhl, F. M. T., 141

Borneo, 176, 191

Brains: warfare as factor in size increase, 4, 106, 163, 249; group action dependent upon, 5; interpret and devise communication, 5, 49, 53, 57; evolution of, 6, 10; required for adjustment to change, 11; size increase during Pleistocene, 11–12, 45, 49; as social instrument, 11, 28, 50; selective force in development of, 11–20, 49–59; size of and intelligence, 11; required for cooperation, 15, 19, 27; required for character judgment, 26, 47; of gorillas, 42; evolved through competition, 43; of australopithecines, 45, 47, 49, 120; effect of predation pressure on, 49–50; nerve cells, 49, 49n.; products of gene interaction, 57; and relation to European increase, 108; effect of polygamy on size of, 116; how evolutionary change produced, 120; variation of mental efficiency during development of, 130; among different races, 133; effect of mobility on growth, 138–139; needed to organize Genghis Khan's empire, 151–153; human versus carnivore rival, 188; realize necessity of global cooperation, 226; gradual increase in ability to cope, 227; primitive, unable to cooperate, 230; current need of aptitudes, 236–237; learning irrationality, 247–248; have ability to learn, 251; control decision on war or peace, 255. *See also* Intelligence

Britain/British, 13–15 *passim*, 52, 65, 68, 79, 95, 98–99, 101, 114, 145, 147, 171, 175–176, 178, 180, 185, 199

British Columbia, 191, 193, 195

Bronze Age, 65

Budongo Forest, 36

Bulgaria, 69

Bulgars, 150

Burial customs, 146, 158–159

Burn, Andrew, 66, 71–72, 79–81

Bushmen, 41, 129, 186, 191, 196–197, 208

CAESAR, JULIUS, 23, 105, 123, 145, 171

Calder, Ritchie, 204

Canaan (Promised Land), 8, 15–17, 35, 76, 86, 151, 217–219, 222–225, 228–229

Canada, 198

Carthage/Carthaginians, 151, 171, 174–175

Caucasians (caucasoid genes), 66, 132–133, 140, 143, 145–146, 148, 176, 184n.

Cavalry. *See* Horses

Celts, 68, 95, 175

Chadwick, John, 68n.

Chariots. *See* Mobility of men

Charlemagne, 115

Cheetahs, 22

Cherokees, 99–101

Childe, Gordon, 63, 71, 184

Chimpanzees, 11, 12, 32–41, 50, 201, 230

Ch'in kingdom, 87–88, 153

China/Chinese, 13, 14, 16, 62, 74, 75, 84–91, 93–94, 102, 115, 132–133, 139–140, 142–153, 171, 175–176, 186; Great Wall, 88–89, 146, 176

Chippewas (Ojibways), 195

Chou dynasty, 86–87

Christians, 115, 235

Churchill, Winston, 18, 179

Cimmerians, 154, 175

City-states, 13–14, 63–64, 83, 168, 216, 234

Civilization, as corrupting force, 63, 133n., 186–187, 190–191, 196, 198–199, 204–205, 214–215, 250–251, 253

Civilizations, 13–14, 17, 102, 139, 149, 168, 171, 173, 213–214, 234, 252

Cleopatra, 123

Climate, 51, 92, 121–122, 125

Commerce (trade), 66, 69–70, 73, 171, 173, 184

Communication (language), 58; required for group action, 5; organized by humans, 4, 6; cooperation requires, 19; how achieved, 19–20; among primates, 30–31; requires brains, 49, 57; linguistic differences, 52–53, 96–97, 127–128; illiteracy, 97, 154; as evidence of human movement, 97, 99; ancestral, 141n.; example of human intellect, 202

Competition, in settling of America, 98

Concubinage, 115

Cook, Capt. James, 177

Coon, Carlton, 35n., 49n., 86–87, 90–91, 119n., 156n., 184, 189, 201, 209n., 244

Cooperation (group action): relation to ferocity, 3; survival depends upon, 3, 5–6, 28, 211, 226; among early humans, 4–6; nonexistent between primitive groups, 4; dependent upon communication, 5; ability of brains to learn, 5–6; among primates, 10; difficult to learn, 15; confers power, 15, 19; requires brains, 15, 19; requires balance with discipline, 26; related to conflict, 58; as inherited ability, 4, 106; advance of, 108; maintained by coercion and obedience in empires, 138–139, 168–169; and mobility, 138–139; large scale, 138; failure to meet demands of, 145; beyond death, 158–159; versus art theory of civilization, 234; necessary at present, 237; present state of, 252–253. See also Peace; Social groups

COOPERATION-FOR-CONFLICT: ferocity produces, 3, 4, 7–8; intergroup, 8, 16, 78, 81–82; as step toward peace, 8–9, 20, 102; at present, 8; evidence of, in early history, 13–20; bestows power, 19; as effective defense, 20, 88; produces biological improvement, 79, 108; in ancient China, 86–87; in building of Great Wall of China, 88–89; possible relation to American immigration, 93; thesis and evidence, 94, 102; Darwin's conception of, 103–105; success in war dependent upon, 105–106; as inherited ability, 106; produces increased Lebensraum and reproduction, 106–109; effect of mobilization on, 138; demand for, among Asian nomads, 149–150; in Genghis Khan's empire, 151–153; in primitive societies, 203, 211–214; dangers of feuds in, 212–213, 231; violence controlled by threat and violence, 214; key to survival, 217; among Hebrew tribes, 217–225, 227–229; demanded by religions, 224–226, 231; hope for change to cooperation-for-survival, 250–255. See also Peace; Social groups

Coordination, biological, 240–242

Cortez, Hernando, 95

Crassus, 23, 144

Crete, 69, 71–72, 142, 171–173

Cro-Magnon man, 13, 150, 206, 209–210

Crow, James F., 117

Cultural evolution, 86, 94, 96, 101, 133, 203, 209n., 234–235, 239–248, 255

Culture: mixtures of, 65; changes in, 67, 210; diffusion of, 85. See also Cultural evolution

Cyrus, 143–144

DANIEL, GLYN, 172

Dardanelles, 83

Darius, 17, 143–144, 161

Dart, Raymond A., 46

Darwin, Charles, 46, 103–106, 108, 187

Defense, 20, 69, 84, 88–89, 188

Denmark/Danes, 171–172, 179

Desborough, V. R., 72–73

Descent of Man (Darwin), 103

De Vore, Irven, 22, 23, 25, 28, 29

Diffusions, 85, 98, 172

Dimeni people, 65

Dinah, 114, 220

Discipline, 26, 103. *See also* Soldiers: disciplined
Disease, 50–51
Displacement, of people, 77, 83
Diversity, human. *See* Genes: diversity of
Dobzhansky, Theodosius, 242
Dogs, 5, 36–37, 39, 124, 201–202, 251
Dorians, 72–73, 76
Drang nach Osten, 249–250
Dravidians, 184, 184n.
Drift. *See* Genes: drift of
Druids, 95
Dutch, 101, 176, 208

EANNATUM, KING, 63
Earthquake theory, 72
Economic institutions, 244
Egypt, 13, 15, 74–79 *passim*, 83, 85, 86, 93, 102, 114, 123, 138, 141–143, 171, 173, 184–185, 212, 218–219, 221
Elamites, 16, 184
Ellis, Havelock, 202
Emotions, and evolution, 61, 77, 79, 130–131
Empires (kingdoms), 74–75, 93–94, 138, 147–148, 153, 252. *See also* Social groups: cohesion
Endocrine systems, 5, 131, 133, 226, 240–241
Enemies. *See* Foreigners
England. *See* Britain
Environment, 108–109, 133, 187, 203, 243
Epic of Man, 183
Equality, among humans, 130–136
Erik Bloody-Axe, 180
Eskimos, 91, 191, 195, 215
Etruscans, 174
Eurasia, 14, 75, 89, 140, 153
Europe/Europeans: 66, 146, 167, 168, 250; Neanderthal and Cro-Magnon men in, 13, 150, 206–210; success in war, 14, 18, 57, 140; increase of and spread of genes, 17–18, 107–108; cities, 56; invasion of North America, 57, 91, 98, 176; Neolithic period, 65; movement of Indo-Europeans in, 76; and population explosions, 86, 88, 93; and Huns, 87n., 89, 148; inbreeding in royal families, 123; horsemen bring genes to, 139, 142, 144–145, 149; language, 141n., and Mongols, 152; and Scythians, 161; and sea flow, 171, 176–178, 181; and Vikings, 178–180; at beginning of second millenium B.C., 185; in Australia, 189, 196–197. *See also individual country entries*; Eurasia; Indo-Europeans

Evolution, 57; works through law of averages, 6; requirements for, 7; pace quickened by cooperation, 8; evidence for theories, 9–10; biological, 20, 88–90, 94, 101–102, 203, 236–237, 239; concentration on individuals, 28; role of disease in, 50–51; basic ingredients of, 61; cultural, 86, 94, 96, 101, 203, 209n., 234–235, 239, 255; Asian influence on, 89, 144, 147–148, 150, 153–154, 175–176; rate of, 91; social, 96, 101–103, 106, 108; moral, 103, 106; result of natural selection, 116, 188; gene recombination produces change in, 117–118; genetic drift theory, 121–127; hopeful results of, 136; effect of mobility on, 137–139, 180; sea as factor in, 175–181; gradual changes in, 187–188, 225

WARFARE THEORY OF: man's capacity for conflict, 3–4; war as complement to peace, 4; war and brain-size increase, 4, 49–59, 163, 249; thesis, 4–9, 19–

Evolution (*Continued*)
20, 57, 94; evidence for, 9–20, 58, 94, 183; arguments against thesis, 17, 103–105; winners produce more offspring, 17, 58, 104–105, 109–110, 135, 252; Australopithecine as social animal, 21–22, 46–57; behavior of monkeys and apes as evidence, 21–43; human killing of own species, 42–43, 135; implications of theory, 58; activity produced by war, 61; population explosion examples as evidence, 62–102; alteration in scale of war, 64; possibility of biological improvement after conflict, 78–79; biological expediency of sacrifice and massacre, 95, 100–101, 158, 235–236; Darwin's conception of, 103–106; importance of increased *Lebensraum* and reproduction, 106–109; polygamy and reproduction, 106, 109–116; connection with genes and human harmony, 170; as opposed to prehistoric peace, 183–214; warfare as religion among primitive tribes, 223–237; interaction of biology and culture, 239–248; expansion toward global cooperation, 250–255. *See also* Cooperation-for-conflict; Evolution; Genes; Land; Mobility; Natural selection; Peace; Population explosions; Warfare

Experience, 251

Extinction, 119, 197

FAITH, 168–169

Famine. *See* Starvation

Ferocity. *See* Cooperation-for-conflict

Feuds, 102, 212–213, 231

Food, 12, 27, 37, 50, 51, 53, 54, 72, 78, 91–92, 99, 101, 121– 122, 125, 135, 187, 193. *See also* Agriculture; Hunting; Starvation

Foreigners (enemies, strangers), 4, 8, 16–17, 20, 31, 47, 52, 58– 59, 64, 70, 148, 154, 155–163, 190, 195, 207–208, 220, 246

Fortifications and walls, 66–67, 71, 80–82, 88–89, 94, 173, 189

Four Thousand Years Ago (Bibby), 184

France/French, 64, 98, 99, 101, 115, 148, 172

Frederick Wilhelm II, 115

Friends (neighbors), 58–59, 162–163, 225

GAULS, 15, 105, 175

Genes, 47, 57; development of brains through action of, 6, 49, 57; variability maintained through recombination, 7, 117–118, 120; distribution of, in war, 17–19, 104–106, 109–110, 135; of successful baboons favored, 26; war-induced changes in, 61; continuity, 67; differences after population explosion, 78–79; human movement and intermixing (gene flow), 88–89, 94, 98; outward flow, from Asia, 89, 144, 147–148, 150, 153–154, 175–176, 180; effects of increased *Lebensraum* on, 106–109, 181; effects of polygamy on, 106, 109–116, 144–145; exchanges of, between tribes, 114; mutated, 116–120; harmful and beneficial features, 118–119; relation to environment, 118–119; drift of, 121–127; diversity of, 122, 126, 129–134, 145; and inbreeding, 124–127; and inheritance, 130–136; defective, 131, 145; determine human capacities, 131–133; exchange of, accelerated by horses, 140,

143–145; mixture of, obscures racial origins, 141; mixture of European and Asian, 140–142, 144–146, 148–149, 174; nomadic sources, 150, 153, 163; connection with human harmony, 169–170; sea flow of, 173–181; overland spread of, 176; spread by Vikings, 177–181; and environment required for life, 203; necessary for warfare, 205; Neanderthal and Cro-Magnon, 209n.; flow of ideas and implements without flow of, 210; wastage of, 229; ability to learn through action of, 251; required for global cooperation, 253

Genghis Khan, 14, 61, 149–153, 162–170, 179, 228

Germany, 87n., 144, 160–161

Gibbons, 36

Gibraltar, Straits of, 176, 178

Global cooperation. See Peace

Gobi Desert, 85, 145–146

Gokstad ship, 178–179

Golden Rule, 7, 20, 225, 237

Goodall, Jane, 32–33, 37–38, 40

Goodrich, L. Carrington, 86

Gorillas, 11, 32, 39–42, 203

Goshen, 142

Goths, 14

Graves, megalithic, 172

Great Wall of China. See China

Greece/Greeks, 14–17 passim, 62, 115, 142, 144, 161, 168, 171, 173–174, 209, 214, 216, 224, 225, 234, 253; build up and effect of population explosions, 65–73, 79–84, 86, 143

Greenland, 180

Groups. See Social groups

HAAKON THE GOOD, 180

Haldane, J. B. S., 115

Hall, K. Ronald L., 22, 23, 24, 29

Harald Fairhair, 180

Harems. See Polygamy

Hart, B. H. Liddell. See Liddell Hart

Harvard-Peabody expedition, 111, 230

Hebrews (Israelites), 14–17, 77–78, 114, 141–142, 174, 214, 217–225, 227–229, 235–236

Herodotus, 146, 154–156, 158–161

Higgs, E. S., 209, 209n.

Himalaya Mts., 85

Hitler, Adolf, 133

Hittites, 16, 74–76, 79, 85–86, 90, 142, 173, 218

Hivites, 114, 218, 220

Hood, Sinclair, 68n.

Horites (Hurrians), 141, 218

Horses, 39, 137–149, 162; cavalry, 143, 146–147, 149, 151, 152

Hot centers. See Population explosions

Howell, F. Clark, 46, 206, 209, 209n., 210

Hsiung Nu, 146–149

Humans: most cooperative animals, 3; ferocity, 3–4; contradictory attitudes of war and peace, 3–4; subhuman, 5, 21; emergence from Pleistocene, 11; interest in "foreigners'" movements, 31; success in war, 41, 104–106; kill own species, 42, 135; death of, 101; nature of, 104–106, 240, 243; differences among, 130–136; as animals, 136, 245; rational and irrational beliefs, 245–247; equipped only for peace, 250–251; values of, 253; capacity for control, 255. See also Animals; Australopithecines; Brains; Genes; Social groups

Hungary, 66, 144–145, 152, 160, 175

Huns, 14, 55, 61, 87n., 89, 138–
139, 145, 147–150, 177–179
passim, 198; Hwang Ho, 87,
87n., 88
Hunting, 97, 185–186, 192–194,
196, 207–208
Huxley, Aldous, 199
Huxley, Sir Julian, 133, 242–243
Hwang Ho River and valley, 84,
87, 87n., 88, 92, 138, 140
Hydrogen bomb, 3, 59, 89, 134,
151, 153, 155, 158, 237, 254–
255
Hyksos invasion, 141–142

ICELAND, 180
Ideas, flow of, 96, 172, 210
Idriess, I. L., 112–113, 232–233
Illyrians, 76
Inbreeding, 121–126
Incas, 14, 93–94, 102, 177, 235
India, 30, 85, 87–89 *passim*, 115,
141n., 142–143, 149, 150, 151,
175–176
Indians, American, 14, 18, 53, 62,
88, 90–102, 108, 114, 129, 139,
155, 171, 191, 193, 195, 208–
209, 244. *See also individual
tribes*
Indo-Europeans (Indo-Aryans),
75, 140–141, 141n., 154, 174,
174n., 218
Indonesians, 87
Indus River and valley, 85, 93,
138, 184
Inferiority. *See* Genes; Equality
Innate behavior, 130–131, 200–
205, 249
Insects, 135
Instinct, 200–201, 244, *See also*
Innate behavior
Intelligence, 11, 51, 54, 107, 133,
136, 201–202, 205. *See also*
Brains
Interacting systems, 241
Interbreeding, 108, 132, 134
Intuition, 200

Invasions; invaders, 65, 66, 68, 73,
76, 141–142, 144, 209–210,
210n.
Ionians, 76
Iran (Persia)/Iranians, 14, 77, 83,
143–144, 147, 153, 164, 166
Ireland, 115, 172, 179–180
Iroquois, 99, 100–102, 194, 225
Isaac, 114, 217
Israelites. *See* Hebrews
Italy, 67, 83, 89, 144, 172–175

JACKSON, STONEWALL, 138
Jacob, 217, 220, 229
Japan, 91, 115, 176, 209, 210n.
Jericho, 189, 223
Jordan River and valley, 141, 218,
222
Joseph, 142, 221
Joshua, 8, 16–17, 73, 86, 187,
223–225, 227–228
Juvaini, 'Ala-ad-Din-Ata-Malik,
164–170

KAINS, 111–112, 231
Kassites, 16, 75
Keith, Sir Arthur, 249
Kellett, E. E., 223
Kenyon, Kathleen, 189
Kepu men, 111
Kipchaks, 150
Knossos, 71–72
Kootenays, 193
Kortlandt, Adriaan, 41
Krakatoa, 74
Kraus, Bertram S., 187
Kurelu tribe, 111–112, 230–231

LACONIA, 80
La Farge, Oliver, 92, 99–101, 196
Lagash, 63–64, 71, 217–218
Land (territory; desirable areas):
competition for, 6, 92; and
Israelites, 15, 221–222, 228;
and Australopithecines, 51–54;
and Sumer, 63–64; and Neolithic farmers, 65; and ancient

Greece, 73–82; and barbarian tribes, 75–77; as cause of war, 92, 115, 222; *Lebensraum*, 106–109, 181, 249; and primitive peoples, 187, 197, 224
Language. *See* Communication
Lapps, 198
Lasker, Gabriel W., 130
Latins, 174–175
Law and order, 138, 153, 166
Leagues, 83
Learning capacity, 130, 205, 229, 247
Lebensraum. *See* Land
Leechman, Douglas, 102, 193–195
Leopards, 11, 22, 38, 41
Lerna, 66–67
"Lethals," 116
Levi, 114, 123, 222
Li people, 87
Liddell Hart, B. H., 152
Life magazine, 183
Linear B tablets, 68n.
Lions, 5, 11, 22, 39, 41, 46, 48–49, 61, 203
Lissner, Ivar, 66, 69, 71
Lorenz, Konrad, 46, 204
Lot, 219
Lucanians, 174–175
Luck, 126–127, 229

McEvedy, Colin, 13, 62
Magyars, 150
Mair, Lucy, 211, 213
Malinowski, Bronislaw, 109
Malta, 172
Mammalian behavior, 201, 251
Man. *See* Humans
Man and Aggression (Montagu), 204
Manchuria, 145
Manus people, 128
Mao-tun, 147
Mason, J. Alden, 93–94, 129
Massacre, 6, 7, 58, 101, 153, 165, 220
Matthiessen, Peter, 111, 128, 231

Medes, 77, 143
Medicine, 244
Mediterranean Sea, 83, 171, 173–175, 178, 218
Melanesians, 87
Menes, 80, 102, 138
Merenpath, Pharoah, 77
Merv, 164–165
Mesopotamia, 16, 21, 62–65, 74, 75, 78, 85, 184, 218, 221
Mexico, 93–96, 98, 108, 176, 234–236
Miao people, 87
Middle East, 78
Migration. *See* Movement, of people, and migration
Military personnel, effective, 14–15, 47
Missionaries, 171–172
Mississippi River, 99
Mitannians, 14, 75
Mobility of men, 137–139; chariots, 69, 71, 139, 142–144 *passim*, 173–174; horses, 137–149, 162; ships, 137–139, 170–181; roads, 138; cavalry, 143, 146–147, 149, 151, 152, 173. *See also* population explosions
Mohicans, 101
Mongoloids, 140, 145–146, 148
Mongols, 14, 55, 140, 150–153, 164–170, 177, 179, 184, 198
Monkeys, 10–11, 21–31, 42, 204–205. *See also* Baboons
Montagu, Ashley, 199, 202, 204, 211, 251
Montezuma II, 95
Moral evolution, 103, 106
Morality (ethics), 199, 225, 230
Morris, Desmond, 188
Moses, 15, 77, 221–222, 231
Mousterians, 207–209, 209n.
Movement, of people, and migration, 74–78, 83, 85, 87–89, 91, 94, 98–99, 121, 127, 171–173. *See also* Population explosions
Mtessa, King, 110

Mugwumps, 101
Muller, H. J., 244
Mumford, Lewis, 199
Murder, 35, 46
Mutation, 116–122
Mycenaeans, 14, 15, 62, 67–73, 173, 224
Mylonas, George, 73
Myths, 200, 211. See Ideas, flow of

NAPOLEON, 221
Narragansets, 101
Natural selection (survival of the fittest), 125; among early humans, 5–6; definition, 7; favors more successful groups, 17, 135; possible forces, 49–59; during stable period, 82; in Aztec empire, 95; Darwin's conception of, 103–105, 108–109; and environment, 108–109; determines course of evolution, 116, 188; after nuclear war, 119; role in brain changes, 120; and genetic diversity, 121, 129–130, 134, 145; interlude of, among Asiatic nomads, 150; rate of, increased by ships, 170, 173; rate increase and land mobility, 174–175; effectiveness of persistent forces, 183; mental potentialities exceed influence of, 236. See also Selective force, in brain development
Nature, 200, 226, 229, 240
Nazis, 156, 249
Neanderthal man, 13, 150, 206–210
Near East, 62, 65, 66, 74–76, 83–85, 93, 139–140, 142, 173, 217. See also individual country entries
Negroes, 108, 132–133, 184, 184n., 252
Nerve cells, 49, 49n.

New Guinea, 52, 65, 67, 80, 88, 93, 111–112, 115, 127–28, 190, 198, 230
New Zealand, 35, 52, 107, 115, 141n.
Nietzsche, Friedrich, 133, 249–250
Nile River and valley, 80, 93, 138
Nishapur, 166
Nomads: rulers descended from, 139, 142; white, in Asia, 140–142; carry caucasoid genes to Europe, 144; Gobi, 145–146; division among Asian, 149; organized by Genghis Khan, 150–153; behavior among, 154–170. See also individual tribes; Genghis Khan
North America, 18, 52, 56–57, 90–102, 107, 142, 150, 155, 176–177, 195
"Northwestern peoples," 72
Norway, 179–180
Nuclear explosions, 245, 255. See also Warfare: nuclear
Nuer tribe, 113–114, 211–213

OFFSPRING: winners produce more, 58, 104–105, 110; in wars, 61; environment a factor in number, 108–109. See also Reproduction
Ohio River, 99
Organization. See Social groups
Ostiaks, 198

PACIFIC OCEAN, 176–177
Paiute Indians, 191–192, 195–197
Paleolithic people, Upper, 207, 209
Palestine, 16, 76, 141, 174
Paranthropus, 119
Parthians, 14, 77, 144, 149
Pax Britannica, 102
Pax Romana, 80, 102
Pazirik tombs, 145–146
Peace: feasibility of, in world, 4,

8, 20, 58–59, 136, 181, 216; complements war, 4; doctrine of prehistoric, 19, 69–72, 88, 150, 156, 181–216, 249; tendencies for, among apes and humans, 38, 40–41, 252; produced by suppression of feuds, 102; global, 130, 133–134, 153, 216, 225–228, 237, 247, 250, 253; connection with genes, 170; philosophy that man equipped only for, 250–251

Pechenegs, 150

Peloponnesus, 66

Pequots, 101

Perigordian era, 209n.

Perioikoi, 81

Persian Empire, 83–84. See also Iran

Personality, 28

Peru, 93, 96, 98, 129, 176, 186, 235

Peterson, Roger Tory, 244

Philistines, 174

Phillips, Eustace D., 139, 144–146

Philosophy, 10, 28

Phocis, 80

Phoenicians, 83–84, 174

Piggott, Stuart, 140

Piracy, 66, 173, 176

Pizarro, Francisco, 235

Pleistocene epoch, 11–13, 46, 90, 194, 197–198, 206–207, 252. See also Australopithecines

Pocahontas, 101

Poland, 151

Political unity, 23, 26, 35, 80–82, 86–87, 95, 97, 244

Polyandry, 109

Polygamy, 18, 106, 109–116, 144

Polygny, 109

Polynesians, 14, 87, 123, 177

Pompey, 23

Population: increases, 81–82, 84, 107–109; shifting of, 87–88, 94; low density, 198; size, 244–245. See also Population explosions

Population explosions: among australopithecines, 54–56; and world expansion, 55–56; hot centers, 56, 62–63, 98, 137, 180, 197, 218; war-induced, 61, 64–65; example of process that leads to, 62–65; and Greece, 65–73, 79–84; of 1200 B.C., 74, 76; causes and results of, 74–79, 81–82, 84, 98; dates of, 75; buildup of, in China, 84–90; and immigration to America, 90–102; in Asia, 150; of Europe, to seas, 176–177, 181; current pressures toward, 252

Portugal, 98, 176

Posture, biped, 45–46, 187–188

Powhatan, 101

Predation pressure, 11, 22, 48–50, 183, 231

Primates, 10–12, 21, 27–30, 36, 42, 47–49, 211. See also Apes; Australopithecines; Monkeys

Primitive people, 112, 230, 240. See also Australopithecines

Prosperity, periods of, 69–70

Protection, 22, 27

Protohominids, 46

Psychology, 10, 28, 242

Punan tribe, 191–192, 196–197

Pygmies, Congo, 129, 190, 197

RACE, 130–134

Raids/raiders, 77, 81, 184, 194–195, 231–232

Rameses II, 77

Rationality and irrationality. See Humans: rational and irrational beliefs of

Rebecca, 114

Recombination of genes. See Genes: variability maintained through recombination

Reed, Stephen W., 128

Regent's Park Zoo, 24

Religion, 15, 168, 171–172, 223–227, 231, 234–237, 244

Reproduction, 12, 134, 219, 221; potential for, 104–106, 108–109. *See also* Genes

Restraint, 251–252. *See also* Baboons; Social groups; Soldiers

Reynolds, Vernon and Frances, 32, 36–38

Rice, Tamara, 144–145

Rivers, 138–139, 171, 231

Rome, 14–15, 17, 67, 75, 79–80, 88, 89, 93–95, 102, 138, 144, 147, 153, 156, 167, 171, 175, 177, 203

Roux, Georges, 63, 75, 85, 189

Russell, W. M. S., 23, 26

Russia, 66, 140, 141n., 144–145, 147, 151, 154, 160–161, 176, 180, 198, 221

Sabines, 174–175

Sacrifice, human, 94–95, 100–101, 158, 235–236

Sakas, 144

Salish Indians, 191, 193–194

Saltation theory, 119–120

Samnites, 174–175

Samoyeds, 198

Samuel, Alan, 69, 173

Sanderson, Ivan T., 31

Santorin, 74

Sarah, 114

Sardinia, 172

Sargon I, 80, 184

Sarmatians, 147, 155

Scandinavia, 160, 175–180, 186. *See also* Denmark, Norway, Sweden

Schaller, George, 39–41

Science; Scientists, 119, 119n., 131, 210, 226, 237, 247

Scythians, 14, 95, 144, 146–147, 154–162, 175, 180

Sea, the 171–181

Sea People (Sea Raiders), 15, 76–77, 86, 143, 173–174, 224

Second millennium B.C., 72, 75, 143, 173, 184–187, 214, 217, 221–222, 228–229

Segregation, 33–34, 56

Selective force, in brain development, 11–20, 49–59. *See also* Natural selection

Semitic populations, 40–42, 174, 217–218

Sex, 7, 11, 23–25, 33, 40, 118, 122

Shaft Grave people, 68–70, 73

Shakespeare, William, 4, 7

Shang dynasty, 16, 85–86, 142

Shechem, 114, 220

Ships, 137–139, 170–181

Siberia/Siberians, 91, 140, 186, 198

Sicily, 83, 172–173, 180

Simeon, 114, 123, 220

Sinai peninsula, 221–222

Sioux tribes, 195

Slavery, 75, 86, 133, 155–157, 175, 194, 249

Smith, Elliot, 113, 190–195, 197–200, 202, 215

Smith, John, 101

Social cohesion. *See* Social groups: cohesion

Social efficiency, 133, 147

Social evolution, 95, 101–103, 106, 108

Social groups: organization, 4, 57; early human, cooperation within, 4–5; intergroup behavior, 4–5, 8, 16, 37, 47–48, 57, 81, 85, 129; requirements for action within, 5; among primates in general, 10–11, 27–30, 36; most powerful as winners, 17, 135; of australopithecines, 22, 47, 52–56; provide protection, 22–23; organization, cooperation and sublimation within, 23; requires balance between discipline and cooperation, 26; importance over individuals, 28, 48, 197; definition, 34–35; functional, 35, 37–

38; segregation, 56, 127–129, 246; more successful prevail, 56–57, 135, 252; that sweep outward from "hot centers," 56–57; development of friction, 64; cohesion, 74–75, 78–80, 82, 86, 93–94, 151, 168, 246, 252; pressures, 76, 78, 84, 98; in Greece and ancient China, 86–87; unity over vast area, 88; growth sequence maintained by force, 94; in Aztec empire, 94–96; among American Indians, 96; as factor in reproduction, 108–109; inbreeding, 122–127; size, past and present, 129; differ genetically, 131, 134; mobilization, 137–138; least cooperative removed by increased mobility, 138; and Hsiung Nu empire, 147; of nomads, organized by Genghis Khan, 150–153, 166–170; effect of fear, 155–159, 220, 231–232; organized into Roman Empire, 175–176; prehistoric interaction among, 194–197; primitive tribes, 211–214, 230–231; interhostility in ancient Near East, 217–218; unity, among Hebrew tribes, 217–225, 227–229; reduction important to enemy, 230; rational and irrational beliefs of, 246–248. *See also* Baboons; Cooperation (group action); Cooperation-for-conflict

Sociology, 10, 242

Soldiers: as killers and intelligent humans, 58; in Shaft Grave era, 70; spread genes, 89, 104–106, 135; disciplined, 103, 105, 206; of Asian nomads, 149

South America, 52, 56, 90–102, 107–108, 141n., 176, 235

Spain/Spaniards, 93, 98, 147, 171, 172, 176, 185, 235

Species: primate behavior with other groups in, 29–31; humans kill own, 42, 135; survival as, 133–134

Squid, 248

Starvation (famine), 7, 51, 58, 186, 218, 221–222

Stele of the Vultures, 63

Stone Age, 91, 197

Sumer/Sumerians, 14, 63, 90, 139, 183, 218, 253

Superiority. *See* Genes: equality

Supernatural, the (abstract; spirits; superstition; unknown), 200, 225–226, 232–236, 239–241, 247

Survival, 5–6, 8, 28, 53, 56, 84, 95, 113, 119, 133–134, 163–164, 211, 217, 225–226, 230–231, 233, 246–247, 255. *See also* Natural selection

Survival of the fittest. *See* Natural selection

Sweden, 199

Syria, 141, 167, 209n.

TASMANIANS, 108, 176

Territorial Imperative, The (Ardrey), 203

Thais, 87

Theology, 10

Thessaly, 66

Third millennium B.C., 66, 184

Thorpe, William H., 236–237

Thraco-Phrygians, 76

Tibet, 145

Tierra del Fuego, 56, 91–92, 191, 203

Tigris-Euphrates, 80, 92

Tiles, House of, 67

Tirmiz, 165

Tocharians, 147

Tools, 32, 46, 53n., 209, 210. *See also* Weapons

Trade. *See* Commerce

Trial, by combat, 212
Tribes: in Greece, 70; hardships and migrations during population explosions, 75, 77–78; hostile, between China and Near East, 85; effect of Aztecs on, 94–95; primitive, 96–97, 233; American Indian, 99; as opposed to individuals, 103–107; treatment of small, by powerful, 114; in New Guinea, 128; division among Asian, 149; annihilation of, 176. *See also* individual tribe entries; Nomads; Social Groups
Tripolye people, 140
Trowell, the Rev. H. S., 115
Turks, 115, 147, 150

UMBRIANS, 174
Umma, 63–64, 71, 217
UNESCO, 130–133
UN Statistical Yearbook, 245
United States, 52
Ur, 218

VAILLANT, GEORGE, 94–95, 234
Values. *See* Humans: values of
Vedda tribe, 197
Ventris, Michael G. F., 68n.
Vermeule, Emily, 65–67, 69–70, 73
Vikings, 14, 18, 55, 66, 95, 138, 159, 171, 177–181, 185
Volsci, 175

WALLS. *See* Fortifications and walls
Wales, 172
Wallis, Wilson, 189
Ward, Russel, 189
Warfare: man's capacity for, 3–4; effect of intergroup cooperation, 8; as selective force, 11–20, 183; nuclear, 9, 119, 136, 228, 252; assumptions about beginning of, 19, 57, 62; destruction of, 20; disrupts army organization, 48; produces activity and change, 61, 64; account of, in first written records, 62; scale of, altered, 64; in early times, 64; growth, 70–73; regarded as immoral, 84; causes, 92; relation to human sacrifice, 94–95, 235–236; among American Indians, 99; success in, 105; effect of horses and ships on, 143; intertribal, 149; innate in human nature, 249; tactics among Asian nomads, 149–150; waged by Genghis Khan, 151–153, 162–170; prisoners of, 155–161, 164; Scythian, 160–162; at sea, 171–174; genes necessary for, 205; current progress against, 254–255. *See also* Evolution, warfare theory of
Washburn, Sherwood L., 28, 46, 204
Wattaia tribe, 230–231
Weapons, 9, 12–13, 32, 46, 53n., 66, 68–71, 93, 96, 99, 107, 143, 145, 147, 152, 187–188, 194, 196, 243, 247, 254–255. *See also* Tools
White, Lancelot Law, 201
"White peril," 108
Whites, 140
Wilderness period, 77–78, 222, 228. *See also* Hebrews
William the Conqueror, 67–68, 179
Williams, Maslyn, 190
Wissler, Clark, 96–98
Women, 75, 78; primitive, 48; as war prizes, 55, 109–110, 115, 135, 161–163, 187, 229; and polygamy, 109–116
World Wars I and II, 148, 249
Wright, Sewall, 121–127, 134
Wu people, 87

XERXES, 17, 143–144

YAHWEH (God), 8, 187, 223, 228
Yao people, 87
"Yellow peril," 108
Yellow Sea, 171
Yenesei River, 140

Yueh Chi tribe, 147–148

ZULUS, 14
Zungaria, 140
Zygote, 203